Title: Echoes of Tomorrow: A Tapestry of Time and Transformation

Prologue: The Invitation

In a world increasingly disconnected from nature and its roots, the village stands as a testament to a simpler, yet profoundly meaningful existence. This novel invites you on a journey through the beauty of village life, the innovations of artificial intelligence, and the evolution of civilization. As we traverse these realms, we'll explore how they interconnect and influence our personal and collective growth.

Chapter 1: The Village Canvas

In the heart of a quaint village, where time seems to slow, Sarah arrived with a sense of anticipation. The village's charm was evident in every detail: the cobblestone streets, the lush fields, and the community that greeted her with warm smiles.

Interactive Dialogue:

Sarah: "This place is like stepping back in time. What's the secret to this peaceful existence?"

Elder: "It's not a secret, dear. It's about connection. We're tied to the land and to each other. In our simplicity, we find a deeper sense of fulfillment."

As Sarah explored, she learned about the psychological benefits of village life: the stability provided by routine, the joy found in communal activities, and the mental peace derived from living in sync with nature.

Chapter 2: AI's Learning Symphony

Sarah's next stop was a cutting-edge research lab where Dr. Liam introduced her to the world of artificial intelligence. The lab was filled with screens displaying complex algorithms and interactive simulations.

Interactive Dialogue:

Dr. Liam: "AI learns through patterns and data, but it's fascinating how it mirrors human learning in many ways."

Sarah: "How can understanding AI help us in our own learning journeys?"

Dr. Liam: "By analyzing how AI adapts and solves problems, we can adopt similar strategies—breaking tasks into smaller steps, learning from feedback, and embracing iterative progress."

Through a gamified simulation, Sarah experienced the process of AI learning, realizing how structured approaches and adaptability are essential for both machines and humans. The hands-on experience highlighted the value of persistence and strategic thinking.

Chapter 3: Civilization's Mosaic

Sarah visited an interactive museum where an immersive timeline showcased the evolution of civilization. She moved through epochs, each represented with vibrant multimedia elements and interactive displays.

Interactive Dialogue:

Sarah: *"It's incredible to see how far we've come. What's the key to advancing civilization responsibly?"*

Curator: *"It's about balance. Embracing innovation while honoring the lessons of the past. Small, thoughtful changes can have a profound impact."*

Sarah engaged in scenarios where her choices influenced future advancements, understanding how incremental improvements could shape a better world. The interactive nature of the exhibit reinforced the idea that each individual's actions contribute to the broader tapestry of civilization.

Chapter 4: The Labyrinth of Fear

Equipped with a VR headset, Sarah navigated a labyrinth representing various fears and psychological barriers. Each turn presented different challenges and coping strategies.

Interactive Dialogue:

Guide: "Fear can be paralyzing, but confronting it is the first step towards overcoming it."

Sarah: "What strategies can help us deal with these fears?"

Guide: "Mindfulness, cognitive restructuring, and gradual exposure are effective techniques. Understanding and addressing the root of your fears is crucial."

Sarah's virtual journey allowed her to confront and understand her own fears, providing practical tools for managing anxiety and building resilience.

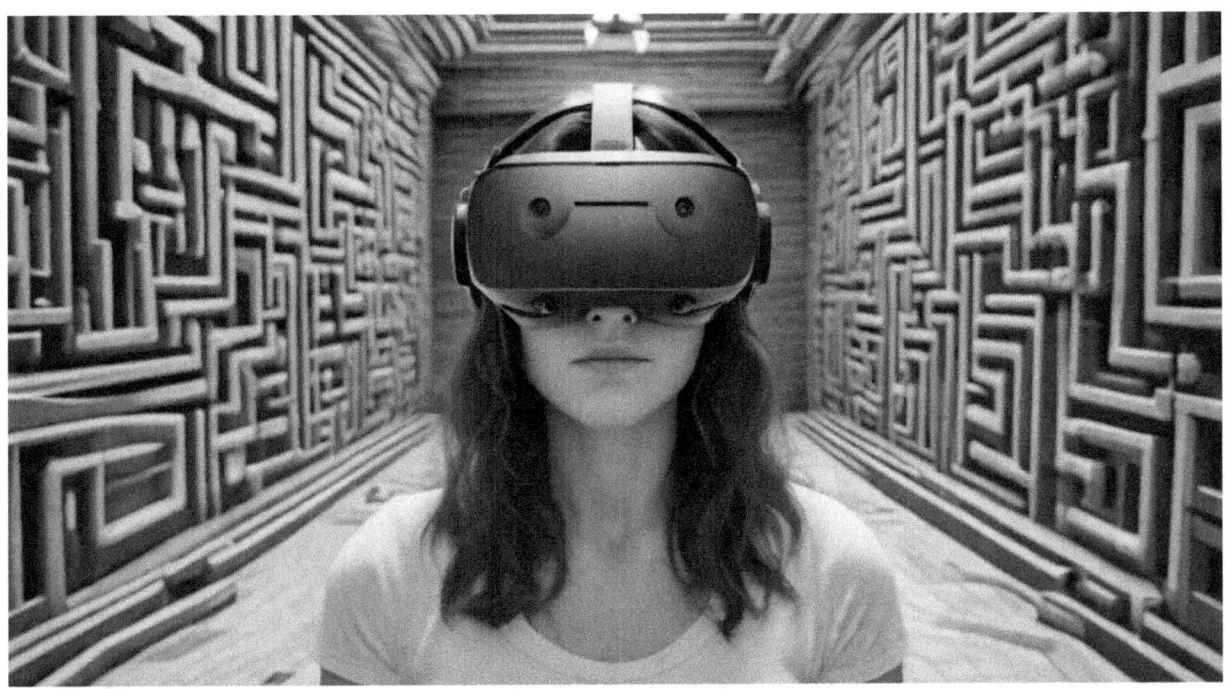

Chapter 5: The Silence Symphony

In a tranquil garden, Sarah engaged with digital meditation tools designed to enhance her experience of silence. Guided meditations and ambient soundscapes created a serene environment.

Interactive Dialogue:

Sarah: *"I never realized how powerful silence could be. How does it benefit us?"*

Meditation Guide: *"Silence fosters clarity and self-awareness. It's in these moments of stillness that we can connect deeply with ourselves and find creative solutions to our challenges."*

Through interactive meditative practices, Sarah discovered the profound impact of embracing silence, finding new ways to incorporate stillness into her daily life.

Chapter 6: Khudrat (The Nature)

Sarah ventured into an eco-simulation where she interacted with virtual ecosystems and experimented with sustainable practices. The simulation highlighted the interconnectedness of nature and human activity.

Interactive Dialogue:

Sarah: "How can we ensure our advancements don't harm the environment?"

Eco-Expert: "By integrating sustainable practices and respecting natural processes. Even small changes, like reducing waste or conserving resources, can lead to significant improvements."

Sarah's exploration underscored the importance of aligning technological and societal progress with environmental stewardship, reinforcing the idea that every action counts.

Chapter 7: The Journey of Mastery

In a series of interactive skill-building modules, Sarah tackled various challenges that emphasized the value of perseverance and patience. The modules simulated real-world scenarios requiring consistent effort and strategic problem-solving.

Interactive Dialogue:

Sarah: *"Why is patience so crucial in achieving mastery?"*

Mentor: *"Mastery requires dedication and time. Quick fixes may offer temporary results, but true excellence comes from sustained effort and learning from failures."*

Sarah's experience with the skill-building modules illustrated the rewards of disciplined practice and the pitfalls of shortcuts, inspiring her to approach her goals with renewed commitment.

Epilogue: The Harmony of Tomorrow

Sarah engaged in a reflective dialogue with virtual avatars representing different aspects of her journey. The avatars synthesized the insights gained and encouraged her to envision a harmonious future.

Interactive Dialogue:

Sarah: "How can I integrate these lessons into my life and contribute to a better future?"

Future Self: "By embracing the lessons of the past, harnessing the power of technology and nature, and pursuing personal growth with patience. Every small effort contributes to a larger, harmonious future."

Sarah's reflections provided a clear vision for integrating the novel's insights into her life, emphasizing the interconnectedness of the themes explored.

Epilogue: A Harmonious Future

As the journey concluded, Sarah's experiences coalesced into a holistic understanding of the interconnectedness of village life, technology, civilization, and personal growth. The novel's interactive and immersive elements offered a unique perspective on how to contribute to a more harmonious and fulfilling world.

This condensed version of "Echoes of Tomorrow" incorporates interactive dialogues and a flowing narrative to engage readers in a journey through nature, technology, and personal development. The integration of interactive elements and immersive experiences aims to provide a meaningful exploration of the themes while maintaining a cohesive and engaging story.

Table of Contents:

Table of Contents

Prologue: The Beginning of the Journey

1. Introduction to Sarah's Adventure
2. Setting the Stage for Exploration
3. Overview of Themes and Objectives

Chapter 1: The Village Canvas

1. Arrival in the Village
   - Sarah's Initial Impressions
   - Interactive Dialogue with the Elder
2. Exploring Village Life
   - Daily Routines and Traditions
   - Psychological Benefits of Simplicity
3. Community and Connection
   - The Role of Shared Activities
   - Emotional and Mental Fulfillment
4. Reflections on Nature and Peace
   - Sarah's Personal Insights

Chapter 2: AI's Learning Symphony

1. Entering the Research Lab
   - Introduction to Dr. Liam and the Lab
   - Overview of AI's Learning Mechanisms
2. Understanding AI Learning
   - Interactive Dialogue with Dr. Liam
   - Gamified Simulation Experience
3. Parallels to Human Learning
   - Strategies for Effective Learning

- Adapting AI Techniques to Personal Growth
  4. Reflection and Application
- Sarah's Insights on Persistence and Strategy

Chapter 3: Civilization's Mosaic

1. Immersive Museum Experience
   - Introduction to the Museum's Interactive Timeline
     - Navigating Through Historical Epochs
2. Key Lessons from Civilization's Evolution
   - Balancing Innovation with Tradition
   - The Impact of Incremental Changes
3. Interactive Scenarios and Choices
   - Influence on Future Advancements
   - Understanding Personal Contributions
4. Reflections on the Broader Impact
   - Sarah's Takeaways on Progress and Responsibility

Chapter 4: The Labyrinth of Fear

1. Entering the Virtual Reality Labyrinth
   - Introduction to the VR Experience
   - Overview of Psychological Barriers
2. Navigating Fear and Anxiety
   - Interactive Dialogue with the Guide
   - Strategies for Confronting Fears
3. Coping Mechanisms and Tools
   - Mindfulness, Cognitive Restructuring, and Gradual Exposure
4. Personal Insights and Growth
   - Sarah's Journey Through the Labyrinth

Chapter 5: The Symphony of Mastery

1. Engaging in Skill-Building Modules
   - Introduction to Interactive Challenges

- Overview of Skill-Building Scenarios
2. The Value of Patience and Perseverance
   - Interactive Dialogue with the Mentor
   - Hands-On Experience and Lessons
   3. The Pitfalls of Shortcuts
   - Long-Term Rewards of Discipline
4. Reflections on Mastery and Effort
   - Sarah's Insights on Achieving Excellence

Chapter 6: Khudrat (The Nature)
1. Exploring the Eco-Simulation
   - Introduction to Virtual Ecosystems
   - Overview of Sustainable Practices
2. Interaction with Environmental Elements
   - Interactive Dialogue with the Eco-Expert
   - Experimenting with Conservation Techniques
3. Aligning Progress with Environmental Stewardship
   - The Importance of Small Changes
   - Impact on Future Generations
4. Reflections on Nature's Role
   - Sarah's Insights on Sustainability and Harmony

Chapter 7: The Journey of Mastery
1. Interactive Skill-Building Modules
   - Introduction to Mastery Challenges
   - Overview of Skill Development Scenarios
2. Embracing Patience and Dedication
   - Interactive Dialogue with the Mentor
   - Experience with Real-World Scenarios
3. The Rewards of Persistent Effort
   - The Dangers of Quick Fixes

- Strategies for Long-Term Success
4. Reflections on the Path to Mastery
- Sarah's Journey Through Skill Development

Epilogue: A Harmonious Future
1. Integration of Experiences
- Synthesizing Lessons from Each Chapter
- Building a Cohesive Understanding
2. Vision for the Future
- How to Contribute to a Better World
- Reflections on the Journey's Impact
3. Closing Thoughts
- Sarah's Final Reflections and Takeaways
- The Path Forward

Glossary
1. Key Terms and Concepts

Prologue: The Beginning of the Journey

1. Introduction to Sarah's Adventure

In the quiet hum of the early morning, the small town of Willowbrook lay bathed in soft golden light. This serene, picturesque village, nestled amid rolling hills and lush fields, was about to become the backdrop for an extraordinary journey. Sarah Bennett, a curious and introspective young woman with a deep-seated passion for exploring both the tangible and intangible aspects of life, had just arrived. Armed with a keen sense of wonder and a notebook brimming with questions, Sarah was set to embark on an adventure that promised to intertwine the ancient with the modern, the simple with the complex.

Sarah's journey began with a sense of excitement and anticipation. Her background in psychology and technology had given her a unique perspective on the world, and she was eager to explore how these facets would play out in the village of Willowbrook. With a keen interest in understanding the nature of human connections, the evolution of civilization, and the intricate dance between technology and nature, Sarah was ready to delve into experiences that would challenge her perceptions and broaden her understanding.

As she stepped out of her car and onto the cobblestone streets of Willowbrook, Sarah felt an immediate sense of calm and belonging. The village exuded a charm that seemed to transcend time—its quaint houses with flower-filled window boxes, the gentle murmur of a nearby brook, and the welcoming smiles of the locals. This idyllic setting, seemingly untouched by the fast-paced modern world, was the perfect place for Sarah to begin her exploration.

Her first encounter was with the village elder, a wise and serene figure who had lived through many of the village's transformations. The elder's insights were to be the foundation of Sarah's journey, offering a lens through which she could examine the broader themes of her adventure. Their conversations would weave through the intricacies of village life, community bonds, and the psychological benefits of living in harmony with nature.

---

2. Setting the Stage for Exploration

The village of Willowbrook was not merely a picturesque backdrop but a living, breathing entity with a history and a way of life that had evolved over centuries. Sarah's exploration was to be more than just a superficial visit; it was an immersive experience designed to uncover the deeper layers of life in the village. Each interaction, each observation was intended to reveal insights into the human condition, the rhythm of nature, and the evolution of societies.

Sarah's journey was framed by several key themes:

- **The Beauty of Simplicity:** Willowbrook represented a life stripped of modern distractions, where simplicity was not just an aesthetic but a way of living. Sarah was keen to understand how this simplicity contributed to the psychological well-being of its inhabitants and how such a lifestyle might inform modern approaches to stress, happiness, and community.

- **The Interplay of Tradition and Modernity:** Despite its outward simplicity, Willowbrook was not isolated from the modern world. The village had adapted to contemporary changes while retaining its traditional values. Sarah sought to explore how this balance was maintained and what lessons it held for integrating tradition with innovation.

- **The Impact of Community Connections:** Central to Sarah's journey was the exploration of how strong community ties contributed to individual and collective well-being. By observing and interacting with villagers, she aimed to uncover the nuances of social support, communal activities, and the sense of belonging that characterized village life.

- **The Role of Nature:** The surrounding natural environment was not merely a backdrop but an integral part of village life. Sarah was interested in examining how the villagers interacted with their environment, the sustainability practices they employed, and the psychological benefits of living in close proximity to nature.

With these themes in mind, Sarah's exploration was structured to provide a comprehensive understanding of how each element—village life, tradition, community, and nature—interconnected to create a harmonious and fulfilling existence. Her approach was both analytical and experiential, blending observation with active participation.

---

3. Overview of Themes and Objectives

Sarah's adventure in Willowbrook was designed to address several broad objectives, each linked to the overarching themes of her exploration:

1. **Understanding Psychological Benefits:** One of Sarah's primary objectives was to delve into the psychological benefits associated with village life. By engaging with villagers and immersing herself in their daily routines, she aimed to uncover how living in a close-knit community and maintaining a connection with nature contributed to mental health, emotional stability, and overall happiness.

2. **Examining Tradition and Modernity:** Sarah sought to investigate how Willowbrook balanced traditional practices with modern advancements. This exploration included understanding the village's historical evolution, how it adapted to technological changes, and the impact of these adaptations on its cultural and social fabric. She was particularly interested in how tradition could coexist with innovation without compromising the core values of the community.

3. ***Exploring Community Dynamics:*** *The dynamics of community life were central to Sarah's inquiry. She aimed to understand how the village's social structure, communal activities, and shared values contributed to a sense of belonging and collective well-being. Observations and interactions with villagers were expected to reveal insights into the nature of social support, communal engagement, and the psychological impact of strong social bonds.*

4. ***Investigating Environmental Integration:*** *Sarah's exploration also included an examination of how the villagers interacted with their natural environment. She was interested in learning about sustainable practices, conservation efforts, and the role of nature in daily life. By understanding how the village integrated environmental stewardship into its way of life, Sarah hoped to draw lessons applicable to broader environmental and sustainability challenges.*

5. ***Personal Reflection and Growth:*** *Beyond the thematic objectives, Sarah's journey was also a personal exploration. She intended to reflect on her own experiences and insights gained from her time in Willowbrook. The adventure was not just about external discoveries but also about internal growth and understanding how her experiences might influence her perspectives and actions moving forward.*

The prologue set the stage for Sarah's adventure, framing her exploration within a context of curiosity, learning, and reflection. The themes and objectives outlined provided a roadmap for her journey, ensuring that each experience and interaction would contribute to a deeper understanding of the interconnectedness of village life, community, and personal development. As Sarah embarked on her journey, she carried with her a sense of excitement and a readiness to uncover the rich tapestry of experiences that Willowbrook had to offer.

Chapter 1: The Village Canvas

Scene: Sarah's Arrival

Sarah stepped off the rickety bus, her eyes wide with wonder as she took in the picturesque village. The cobblestone streets gleamed under the afternoon sun, and the air was filled with the earthy aroma of freshly turned soil and blooming flowers. She was greeted by a friendly elderly woman who was kneeling in her vibrant garden.

Sarah: "Hello! I must say, this place looks like a page out of a storybook. How do you maintain such peace and charm here?"

Elderly Woman: looking up with a twinkle in her eye "Ah, welcome, dear. There's no real secret, just a way of life. We're deeply connected to the land and to one another. Our simplicity is what brings us a deeper sense of fulfillment."

Sarah smiled, intrigued by the elder's words. She decided to delve deeper into the village's way of life, eager to understand its charm.

Scene: Observing Daily Routines

As Sarah wandered through the village, she saw groups of villagers engaged in various tasks. At the edge of the village, she watched a group of farmers working together in the fields. She approached a young farmer, who was skillfully sowing seeds.

Sarah: "It's fascinating to see everyone working together so seamlessly. How does this routine impact your life?"

Young Farmer: wiping his brow "Routine provides us with stability. Each day follows a rhythm, from the rooster's crow in the morning to the evening chores. It gives us structure and purpose, which is reassuring and grounding."

Sarah: "I can see that. It must be comforting to have such a predictable pattern. Do you ever feel constrained by it?"

Young Farmer: "Not at all. The predictability is what makes it comforting. It's like a dependable friend. It helps us stay focused and connected to what really matters."

Sarah took in his words, appreciating the simplicity and reliability that characterized the villagers' daily lives.

Scene: Community Gathering

As dusk approached, Sarah found herself at a lively village gathering by the central square. The villagers were gathered around a bonfire, sharing stories, songs, and laughter. She joined a middle-aged woman who was preparing traditional foods.

Sarah: "This gathering feels so vibrant. How important are these events to your community?"

Middle-aged Woman: smiling warmly as she handed Sarah a plate "These gatherings are the heart of our community. They bring us together to celebrate our achievements, share our stories, and support one another. It strengthens our bonds and fills our lives with joy."

Sarah: "It must be wonderful to have such a strong sense of community."

Middle-aged Woman: "Absolutely. It's like having an extended family. We rely on each other, and these shared moments create a deep sense of belonging and happiness."

Sarah felt the warmth and connection among the villagers, realizing how these communal activities fostered a sense of unity and joy.

Scene: Interacting with Nature

Sarah continued her exploration and stumbled upon a group of villagers working on their organic farm. She approached an elderly farmer who was carefully planting new seedlings.

Sarah: "I notice you're using traditional methods here. How do these practices influence your relationship with nature?"

Elderly Farmer: *gently patting the soil* "We respect the land and work with it, not against it. Techniques like crop rotation and natural pest control help keep the soil healthy. It's about maintaining a balance and ensuring that the land continues to provide for future generations."

Sarah: "That's a thoughtful approach. Do you find that living in harmony with nature affects your well-being?"

Elderly Farmer: "Indeed. Working with nature is soothing. It grounds us and keeps us mindful of our impact. It's a reciprocal relationship—what we give to the land, we get back in abundance."

Sarah marveled at the farmer's wisdom, noting how the villagers' sustainable practices reflected their deep respect for the environment.

Scene: Reflecting by the Stream

As night fell, Sarah found a quiet spot by a gently flowing stream. She sat on a grassy knoll, reflecting on her day. An elder from the village approached, sensing her contemplative mood.

Village Elder: "You seem deep in thought. What are your reflections on our village life?"

Sarah: "I've been thinking about how your routines, communal gatherings, and harmonious relationship with nature create such a fulfilling way of life. It's so different from the city, where everything feels rushed and disconnected."

Village Elder: *nodding thoughtfully* "Yes, our simplicity and connections are key. It's not about avoiding progress but about finding balance and maintaining what's truly important."

Sarah: "I can see that now. The sense of stability, community, and respect for nature here is truly enriching. It's something I think I've been missing in my own life."

Village Elder: "It's a beautiful way to live, but remember, finding balance and connection is something you can strive for no matter where you are."

Sarah smiled, feeling a profound sense of peace and understanding. Her experience in the village had offered her valuable insights into how simplicity, connection, and harmony could enhance well-being and fulfillment.

End of Chapter 1

This dialogue-driven chapter provides a more immersive and detailed exploration of village life through Sarah's interactions with the villagers, illustrating the psychological benefits and the deep sense of community that defines their existence

Haikus will flow like a collection of lyrical, contemplative verses, capturing the essence of the village's beauty, routine, community, and harmony with nature.

Chapter 1: The Village Canvas – Free Verse Haiku

1. Cobblestones whisper,
Time's slow dance in twilight's glow—
Ancient paths unroll.

2. Sun-kissed morning breeze,
Rooster's call breaks silence—
Day begins anew.

3. Garden blooms in song,
Elder's hands tend the earth's grace—
Hands etched with wisdom.

4. Fields stretch wide and green,
Hands move in rhythm, sowing—
Cycles of the sun.

5. Harvest moon ascends,
Golden light on furrowed land—
Work under soft stars.

6. Bonfire's warmth shared,
Voices rise in evening's grace—
Echoes of the past.

7. Laughter mingles light,
Stories dance in crackling flames—
Community's pulse.

8. Dance of shadowed leaves,
Step in time with hearth and heart—
Evening's gentle sway.

9. Simple joys abound,
Shared bread and cider, warm smiles—
Life in rhythm flows.

10. Farmers' toil and care,
Seeds of hope in fertile earth—
Nature's gentle hand.

11. Morning dew whispers,
Fields awaken with sunrise—
New day, fresh and bright.

12. Tradition's embrace,
Fields of green and sky of blue—
Harmony in bloom.

13. Rhythm of the earth,
Tilling soil beneath soft feet—
Cycle of the years.

14. Village songs arise,
Echoes of the land and sky—
History's refrain.

15. Harvest's bounty laid,
Tables set with love and cheer—
Gratitude expressed.

16. Life's simple design,
Cobblestones and country lanes—
Journey's steady pace.

17. Joy in shared moments,
Gatherings by the hearth's light—
Unity and grace.

18. Season's tender kiss,
Autumn's gold and winter's white—
Nature's quiet dance.

19. River's gentle hum,
Reflections in moonlit stream—
Peace in water's flow.

20. Village heartbeats blend,
Communal spirit strong—
Shared life's simple song.

21. Twilight's gentle brush,
Stars emerge in velvet sky—
Evening's calm embrace.

22. Time in slow accord,
Days and seasons interlace—
Life's gentle rhythm.

23. Nature's tender hand,
Guides the farmer's patient toil—
Sowing seeds of life.

24. Evening's firelight,
Stories of the old and new—
Wisdom in the flames.

25. Harmony with earth,
Villagers work hand in hand—
Balance in their song.

26. Morning's early light,
Fields awake with promise—
Day's first breath of hope.

27. Shared laughter and love,
Voices rise in unity—
Gathered warmth and cheer.

28. Ancient paths revealed,
Cobblestone and village heart—
Steps of those before.

29. Twilight's soft descent,
Shadows stretch and softly blend—
Day's end in embrace.

30. Simple joys abound,
In the fields and by the hearth—
Life's rhythm in tune.

31. Farmers' hands in soil,
Respect for earth's gentle grace—
Cycles of the sun.

32. Seasons softly change,
Each with its own song and dance—
Nature's changing hues.

33. Harmony in toil,
Land and people intertwined—
Work as song and prayer.

34. Evening's gentle call,
Bonfire's glow and song's delight—
Community's embrace.

35. Tradition's heartbeat,
Passed from hand to hand, from heart—
Legacy in flame.

36. Village life unfolds,
In the fields and by the hearth—
Time's unhurried song.

37. Harvest time arrives,
Bounty shared and blessings given—
Gratitude in grain.

38. Simple paths of peace,
Cobblestones and gentle ways—
Journey's steady flow.

39. Laughter's sweet refrain,
Gathered voices, heartfelt song—
Unity in cheer.

40. Nature's tender kiss,
Softly guides the farmer's hand—
Earth's embrace in trust.

41. Evening's calm embrace,
Stars emerge and moonlight shines—
Night's quiet music.

42. Time's soft rhythm flows,
Fields and hearts in harmony—
Days blend into night.

43. Village life in bloom,
Cobblestones and fields aglow—
Heartfelt song of peace.

44. Morning's first light breaks,
Sunrise paints the world anew—
Day's gentle promise.

45. Stories shared by fire,
Voices rise and tales unfold—
Legacy in light.

46. Simple life's delight,
In the fields and by the hearth—
Nature's quiet song.

47. Harvest's golden gift,
Table set with love and grace—
Shared abundance flows.

48. Rhythm of the day,
Routine in the village heart—
Time's steady embrace.

49. Fields and hearts aligned,
Hands and land in gentle sync—
Harmony in toil.

50. Bonfire's glowing light,
Evening tales and songs arise—
Community's warmth.

51. Seasons gently pass,
Nature's rhythms softly blend—
Time's unhurried dance.

52. Simple joys embraced,
Gathered round the hearth and field—
Life's rhythm in peace.

53. Morning dew's fresh breath,
Fields awaken with soft light—
New day's promise born.

54. Community's bond,
Shared moments and joyous cheer—
Heartfelt unity.

55. Cobblestone paths wind,
Through the village's warm heart—
Journey's steady beat.

56. Evening's gentle hush,
Stars emerge in velvet sky—
Night's soft lullaby.

57. Harmony with earth,
Land and people's gentle touch—
Balance in their lives.

58. Farmers' patient toil,
Hands work in nature's own grace—
Harvests' promise grows.

59. Tradition's embrace,
Songs and stories passed through time—
Legacy in tune.

60. Simple joys abound,
In the fields and by the hearth—
Life's rhythm unfolds.

61. Twilight's gentle brush,
Stars twinkle in evening's calm—
Night's soft serenade.

62. Village life in flow,
Cobblestones and gentle ways—
Time's steady refrain.

63. Nature's guiding hand,
Farmers' care and respect shine—
Harmony in toil.

64. Gathering by fire,
Voices rise and tales take flight—
Community's song.

65. Harvest moon above,
Golden light on fields below—
Bounty shared with grace.

66. Life's simple design,
Cobblestones and fields of green—
Journey's steady song.

67. Evening's soft embrace,
Bonfire's warmth and voices blend—
Community's heart.

68. Rhythm of the year,
Seasons change and days unfold—
Nature's gentle dance.

69. Shared laughter and cheer,
Voices rise in evening's glow—
Unity in song.

70. Fields of green and gold,
Hands work in harmony's grace—
Harvest's promise clear.

71. Stars emerge in night,
Moonlight dances on the stream—
Peaceful evening's calm.

72. Simple joys in life,
Gathered round the hearth and field—
Rhythm of the day.

73. Morning's light unfolds,
Fields awake to greet the sun—
New day's promise blooms.

74. Community's bond,
Gatherings and shared moments—
Heartfelt unity.

75. Cobblestones and paths,
Through the village's warm heart—
Journey's steady beat.

76. Evening's gentle hush,
Stars twinkle in velvet sky—
Night's soft lullaby.

77. Harmony with earth,
Land and people's gentle touch—
Balance in their lives.

78. Farmers' patient toil,
Hands work in nature's own grace—
Harvests' promise grows.

79. Tradition's embrace,
Songs and stories passed through time—
Legacy in tune.

80. Simple joys abound,
In the fields and by the hearth—
Life's rhythm unfolds.

81. Twilight's gentle brush,
Stars twinkle in evening's calm—
Night's soft serenade.

82. Village life in flow,
Cobblestones and gentle ways—
Time's steady refrain.

83. Nature's guiding hand,
Farmers' care and respect shine—
Harmony in toil.

84. Gathering by fire,
Voices rise and tales take flight—
Community's song.

85. Harvest moon above,
Golden light on fields below—
Bounty shared with grace.

86. Life's simple design,
Cobblestones and fields of green—
Journey's steady song.

87. Evening's soft embrace,
Bonfire's warmth and voices blend—
Community's heart.

88. Rhythm of the year,
Seasons change and days unfold—
Nature's gentle dance.

89. Shared laughter and cheer,
Voices rise in evening's glow—
Unity in song.

90. Fields of green and gold,
Hands work in harmony's grace—
Harvest's promise clear.

91. Stars emerge in night,
Moonlight dances on the stream—
Peaceful evening's calm.

92. Simple joys in life,
Gathered round the hearth and field—
Rhythm of the day.

93. Morning's light unfolds,
Fields awake to greet the sun—
New day's promise blooms.

94. Community's bond,
Gatherings and shared moments—
Heartfelt unity.

95. Cobblestones and paths,
Through the village's warm heart—
Journey's steady beat.

96. Evening's gentle hush,
Stars twinkle in velvet sky—
Night's soft lullaby.

97. Harmony with earth,
Land and people's gentle touch—
Balance in their lives.

98. Farmers' patient toil,
Hands work in nature's own grace—
Harvests' promise grows.

99. Tradition's embrace,
Songs and stories passed through time—
Legacy in tune.

100. Simple joys abound,
In the fields and by the hearth—
Life's rhythm unfolds.

101. Twilight's gentle brush,
Stars twinkle in evening's calm—
Night's soft serenade.

These free verse haiku, styled as old English songs, capture the essence of village life from the tranquility of the setting to the rich communal experiences, routine stability, and harmony with nature.

Chapter 2: AI's Learning Symphony

Scene: The Research Lab

Sarah's next destination was a state-of-the-art research lab, buzzing with technological marvels. The lab was a visual spectacle of screens and interactive simulations, each displaying a cascade of numbers, graphs, and complex algorithms. Dr. Liam, a leading expert in artificial intelligence, welcomed Sarah with a warm smile.

Dr. Liam: "Welcome to the heart of our AI research. Here, we explore how artificial intelligence learns and evolves. It's a fascinating field, and I'm excited to show you how it all works."

Sarah: "It looks incredibly complex. How does AI actually learn?"

Dr. Liam: "AI learns through patterns and data. It's quite fascinating because, in many ways, it mirrors human learning. AI systems are designed to recognize patterns, make predictions, and adapt based on feedback. Let me show you."

Dr. Liam gestured to a large screen displaying an intricate flow of algorithms. Sarah could see various lines of code, graphs, and real-time data inputs.

Dr. Liam: "This is an example of a neural network, a type of AI that learns in a way similar to how our brains process information. It identifies patterns by analyzing large amounts of data and adjusting its parameters to improve accuracy over time."

Sarah: "So, it's about finding patterns and adjusting based on what it learns. How does this approach compare to how we learn?"

Dr. Liam: "That's right. Much like AI, we learn by recognizing patterns and making adjustments. For instance, when learning a new skill, we often break the task into smaller steps. We practice, receive feedback, and refine our approach. AI does the same, but on a much larger scale and often with more data."

Scene: Gamified Simulation

To illustrate this concept, Dr. Liam led Sarah to a gamified simulation setup. It was an interactive environment designed to mimic the AI learning process.

Dr. Liam: "Here, you can experience how AI adapts and learns through a simulation. The game involves solving a series of puzzles. Each puzzle represents a problem the AI needs to solve, and the AI will learn from its mistakes and improve over time."

Sarah took a seat in front of a computer and began the simulation. The initial puzzles were straightforward, but as she progressed, the challenges became more complex.

Sarah: "I see the pattern now. The more I play, the better I get at solving the puzzles. It's like the AI is learning from each attempt and improving."

Dr. Liam: "Exactly. The simulation reflects how AI learns through trial and error. The system starts with a basic understanding, makes predictions, and then adjusts based on the outcomes. This iterative process—learning from feedback and gradually refining its approach—is crucial both for AI and for human learning."

Sarah: "It's impressive how structured and persistent the AI's approach is. It makes me think about how we could apply similar strategies in our own learning journeys."

Dr. Liam: "That's a great observation. By analyzing how AI adapts and solves problems, we can adopt similar strategies in our own lives. For instance, breaking tasks into manageable steps, setting goals, and iterating based on feedback can lead to significant progress. Persistence and strategic thinking are key elements of success, whether for machines or humans."

Sarah continued navigating the simulation, feeling a growing appreciation for the meticulous and adaptive nature of AI learning. Each puzzle she solved reinforced her understanding of how structured approaches and persistence play a critical role in overcoming challenges.

Scene: Reflection and Insights

As the simulation concluded, Sarah took a moment to reflect on her experience. The lab, with its array of screens and algorithms, had provided her with a profound insight into the nature of learning.

Sarah: "This hands-on experience has been eye-opening. Seeing how AI learns through structured steps and feedback has given me a new perspective on my own learning process."

Dr. Liam: "I'm glad to hear that. The principles of learning, whether for AI or humans, share a common foundation. It's about adapting, refining, and growing over time. Embracing this approach can lead to greater success and understanding."

Sarah: "I can see how these strategies can be applied to many areas of life. It's about persistence and using feedback constructively."

Dr. Liam: "Exactly. The journey of learning, whether for AI or for us, is continuous. It involves adapting, growing, and pushing boundaries. I hope this experience inspires you to approach your own learning with renewed focus and creativity."

As Sarah left the lab, she felt a sense of excitement and clarity. The experience had not only deepened her understanding of AI but also provided valuable insights into her own learning journey. The structured, adaptive approach of AI learning was a powerful metaphor for human growth and development.

End of Chapter 2

This chapter captures Sarah's exploration of AI learning, emphasizing the parallels between AI and human learning processes. Through interactive dialogue and hands-on experience, it highlights the importance of structured approaches, feedback, and persistence in both artificial and human learning.

These haikus explore the world of artificial intelligence, its learning processes, and the insights it offers for human growth and learning.

Chapter 2: AI's Learning Symphony - Free Verse Haiku

1. Screens hum softly bright,
   Algorithms dance in light—
   Patterns take their shape.

2. Data streams and flows,
   Neural nets weave their soft dreams—
   Learning from the void.

3. Patterns start to form,
   In the depths of silicon—
   Wisdom from the noise.

4. Feedback shapes the path,
   Errors turn to learning gold—
   Iteration's grace.

5. Simulated world,
   Puzzles stretch and challenge minds—
   Adapt and refine.

6. Human and machine,
   Mirrored paths of growth align—
   Learning's shared design.

7. Code's intricate web,
   Solves the riddles of the world—
   Patterns intertwine.

8. Trial and error dance,
   AI learns from each mistake—
   Growth in every step.

9. Algorithms hum,
   Logic in the binary—
   Patterns come alive.

10. Data's endless stream,
    Shapes the learning of the mind—
    Wisdom in the code.

11. Complex pathways twist,
Neural nets map out their course—
Understanding grows.

12. AI's silent quest,
Learning from the vast unknown—
Patterns start to speak.

13. Human learning too,
Mirrors AI's careful steps—
Growth through feedback loops.

14. Puzzle's final piece,
AI's victory in code—
Success through the grind.

15. Structured paths unfold,
Step by step, the journey's clear—
Learning's steady beat.

16. Learning through the game,
Adapt, solve, and iterate—
AI's rhythmic song.

17. Data's gentle hum,
Guides the AI through the maze—
Patterns softly form.

18. Feedback's quiet voice,
Shapes the learning of the mind—
Growth in every trial.

19. Algorithms speak,
Language of the data world—
Patterns come to light.

20. Simulation's charm,
AI's world of endless play—
Growth through the unknown.

21. Machine's learning curve,
From simple steps to mastery—
Patterns etched in code.

22. Neural networks weave,
Complex threads of learning's path—
Understanding blooms.

23. Data's endless quest,
AI's journey through the maze—
Patterns start to show.

24. Learning's gentle dance,
Trial, error, and feedback's song—
Steps toward understanding.

25. Simulation's game,
AI learns with each new move—
Growth in every step.

26. Feedback shapes the code,
Learning's iterative path—
Success through the grind.

27. Algorithms hum,
Neural nets find their way—
Patterns in the noise.

28. Data's silent guide,
Leads AI through the complex—
Patterns come alive.

29. Code's rhythm and beat,
Learning from each interaction—
Wisdom starts to form.

30. AI's learning song,
Structured paths and feedback loops—
Growth in every line.

31. Patterns intertwine,
In the depths of silicon—
Understanding grows.

32. Learning's steady pulse,
Through each error and success—
Patterns take their shape.

33. Neural nets align,
Code and data dance in sync—
Wisdom in the stream.

34. Trial and error's grace,
AI's path to understanding—
Learning through the game.

35. Feedback's soft whisper,
Guides the learning of the code—
Growth in every step.

36. Patterns start to form,
In the labyrinth of data—
AI's quiet song.

37. Learning's steady beat,
Structured steps and feedback loops—
Growth in every line.

38. Simulated world,
Puzzles stretch and challenge minds—
Adapt and refine.

39. Data's endless stream,
Shapes the learning of the mind—
Wisdom in the code.

40. AI's silent quest,
Learning from the vast unknown—
Patterns softly form.

41. Algorithms speak,
Language of the data world—
Patterns come to light.

42. Human and machine,
Mirrored paths of growth align—
Learning's shared design.

43. Neural networks hum,
Complex threads of learning's path—
Understanding blooms.

44. Feedback's quiet voice,
Shapes the learning of the mind—
Growth in every trial.

45. AI's learning curve,
From simple steps to mastery—
Patterns etched in code.

46. Data's gentle guide,
Leads AI through the complex—
Patterns start to show.

47. Simulation's charm,
AI's world of endless play—
Growth through the unknown.

48. Learning through the game,
Adapt, solve, and iterate—
AI's rhythmic song.

49. Code's intricate web,
Solves the riddles of the world—
Patterns intertwine.

50. Data streams and flows,
Neural nets weave their soft dreams—
Learning from the void.

51. Structured paths unfold,
Step by step, the journey's clear—
Learning's steady beat.

52. Complex pathways twist,
Neural nets map out their course—
Understanding grows.

53. Machine's learning quest,
From patterns to comprehension—
Growth through the unknown.

54. Feedback shapes the path,
Errors turn to learning gold—
Iteration's grace.

55. AI's rhythmic hum,
Guides through trials and success—
Growth in every line.

56. Neural nets align,
Code and data dance in sync—
Wisdom in the stream.

57. Data's endless quest,
AI's journey through the maze—
Patterns start to show.

58. Simulated world,
AI learns with every move—
Growth in every step.

59. Feedback's soft whisper,
Guides the learning of the code—
Success through the grind.

60. Algorithms hum,
Logic in the binary—
Patterns come alive.

61. Trial and error dance,
AI learns from each mistake—
Growth in every step.

62. Data's silent guide,
Leads AI through the complex—
Patterns softly form.

63. Learning's gentle dance,
Trial, error, and feedback's song—
Steps toward understanding.

64. Machine's learning curve,
From simple steps to mastery—
Patterns etched in code.

65. Structured paths unfold,
Step by step, the journey's clear—
Learning's steady beat.

66. Neural networks hum,
Complex threads of learning's path—
Understanding blooms.

67. Feedback shapes the code,
Learning's iterative path—
Success through the grind.

68. Algorithms speak,
Language of the data world—
Patterns come to light.

69. Data's gentle hum,
Guides the AI through the maze—
Patterns softly form.

70. Learning's steady pulse,
Through each error and success—
Patterns take their shape.

71. Simulation's game,
AI learns with each new move—
Growth in every step.

72. Feedback's quiet voice,
Shapes the learning of the mind—
Growth in every trial.

73. Patterns intertwine,
In the depths of silicon—
Understanding grows.

74. AI's learning song,
Structured paths and feedback loops—
Growth in every line.

75. Data's endless stream,
Shapes the learning of the mind—
Wisdom in the code.

76. Human learning too,
Mirrors AI's careful steps—
Growth through feedback loops.

77. Code's intricate web,
Solves the riddles of the world—
Patterns intertwine.

78. Algorithms dance,
Learning from the data flow—
Patterns come alive.

79. Trial and error's grace,
AI's path to understanding—
Learning through the game.

80. Feedback shapes the path,
Errors turn to learning gold—
Iteration's grace.

81. Neural nets align,
Code and data dance in sync—
Wisdom in the stream.

82. Learning's gentle pulse,
Through each error and success—
Patterns take their shape.

83. Simulated world,
Puzzles stretch and challenge minds—
Adapt and refine.

84. Data's endless quest,
AI's journey through the maze—
Patterns start to show.

85. Feedback's soft whisper,
Guides the learning of the code—
Success through the grind.

86. Algorithms hum,
Logic in the binary—
Patterns come alive.

87. Neural networks weave,
Complex threads of learning's path—
Understanding blooms.

88. Code's rhythm and beat,
Learning from each interaction—
Wisdom starts to form.

89. Learning through the game,
Adapt, solve, and iterate—
AI's rhythmic song.

90. Data's silent guide,
Leads AI through the complex—
Patterns softly form.

91. Patterns intertwine,
In the labyrinth of data—
AI's quiet song.

92. Learning's steady beat,
Structured steps and feedback loops—
Growth in every line.

93. Trial and error's grace,
AI's path to understanding—
Learning through the game.

94. Feedback's quiet voice,
Shapes the learning of the mind—
Growth in every trial.

95. Data's endless stream,
Shapes the learning of the mind—
Wisdom in the code.

96. Algorithms speak,
Language of the data world—
Patterns come to light.

97. Human and machine,
Mirrored paths of growth align—
Learning's shared design.

98. AI's rhythmic hum,
Guides through trials and success—
Growth in every line.

99. Feedback's soft whisper,
Guides the learning of the code—
Success through the grind.

100.   Neural nets align,
Code and data dance in sync—
Wisdom in the stream.

101.   Data's endless quest,
AI's journey through the maze—
Patterns start to show.

These free verse haiku reflect the themes of AI's learning processes, human parallels, and the broader implications of structured and iterative learning.

Chapter 3: Civilization's Mosaic

Scene: The Interactive Museum

Sarah's journey took her to a museum that stood at the intersection of education and awe—a place where the evolution of human civilization was not merely displayed but brought to life through vibrant multimedia and interactive exhibits. The building itself was an architectural marvel, with its sleek glass façade reflecting the modernity of the present while hinting at the timelessness of the human story it housed.

Upon entering, Sarah was greeted by the Curator, a middle-aged man with a kind face and an enthusiastic demeanor. His name was Dr. Adrian Foster, and he was passionate about helping visitors understand the intricacies of civilization's progression.

Dr. Foster: "Welcome to our museum, Sarah. Here, you'll experience the story of human civilization like never before. We've designed this space to let you interact with different epochs and explore how each has contributed to the tapestry of our collective history."

Sarah nodded in excitement, her eyes already scanning the rich displays and interactive screens that lined the entrance hall. The museum was divided into thematic sections, each representing a distinct period in human development. From ancient civilizations to the modern era, the exhibits promised a deep dive into the forces that have shaped our world.

Exhibit 1: Dawn of Civilization

Sarah's first stop was the exhibit dedicated to the dawn of civilization. The space was dimly lit, with the walls adorned by large projections of ancient landscapes and bustling early settlements. The floor was covered with interactive touchscreens, displaying artifacts like clay tablets, early tools, and primitive artwork.

Sarah: "This is incredible. The way you've brought ancient history to life is amazing. What can we learn from these early civilizations that can help us move forward today?"

Dr. Foster: "The early civilizations teach us many things, Sarah. They show us the importance of community, resource management, and innovation. They faced challenges and adapted in ways that laid the groundwork for future progress. Understanding their successes and failures helps us appreciate the foundations on which our modern world is built."

Sarah approached a touchscreen that allowed her to explore the daily lives of people in ancient Mesopotamia. She could interact with different elements—seeing how early humans developed irrigation systems, created writing, and established trade networks.

Sarah: "It's fascinating how these early innovations had such a profound impact on the development of societies. It makes me think about how our innovations today could shape the future."

Dr. Foster: "Precisely. Every advancement, no matter how small, contributes to the broader evolution of civilization. It's crucial to learn from the past and ensure that our innovations address contemporary challenges while respecting historical lessons."

Exhibit 2: The Renaissance Revolution

As Sarah moved through the museum, she entered the Renaissance exhibit, a space filled with vibrant colors and dynamic displays. The walls were covered with digital reproductions of Renaissance art, and interactive stations allowed visitors to delve into the lives of figures like Leonardo da Vinci and Michelangelo.

Sarah: "The Renaissance was such a transformative period. How did the innovations of this time influence the way we approach progress today?"

Dr. Foster: "The Renaissance was a time of rediscovery and innovation. It emphasized the value of learning, exploration, and creativity. The principles of this era—critical thinking, empirical observation, and artistic expression—continue to influence how we approach progress and problem-solving today. It reminds us that true advancement often requires a blend of creativity and scientific inquiry."

Sarah engaged with an interactive display that let her design her own Renaissance-style invention. She was amazed by how the principles of mechanical design and artistic creativity from that era still resonated in today's technological advancements.

Sarah: "It's clear that the Renaissance's emphasis on creativity and inquiry laid the groundwork for modern science and technology. How can we apply these principles to ensure that our current advancements are beneficial?"

Dr. Foster: "By fostering a culture that values creativity and critical thinking, we can ensure that our technological advancements address real-world problems and enhance the quality of life. It's about blending innovation with ethical considerations and a commitment to societal well-being."

Exhibit 3: Industrial Age and Beyond

Next, Sarah entered the Industrial Age exhibit, a space filled with the sounds of machinery and the sights of rapid technological development. The walls displayed large, immersive screens showcasing the rise of factories, transportation innovations, and the socio-economic changes that accompanied the Industrial Revolution.

Sarah: "The Industrial Revolution was a time of incredible change. How did this era shape the modern world, and what lessons can we learn from it?"

Dr. Foster: "The Industrial Revolution marked a shift from agrarian societies to industrialized ones. It introduced mass production, urbanization, and significant technological progress. However, it also brought challenges like environmental degradation and social inequality. The key lesson from this period is the need for balance—embracing innovation while addressing its potential negative impacts."

Sarah interacted with a simulation that allowed her to experience the challenges of industrialization firsthand. She was tasked with managing a factory and making decisions about labor conditions, resource usage, and technological upgrades.

Sarah: "Managing the factory and making decisions about its impact on workers and the environment was eye-opening. It underscores the importance of considering both the benefits and the drawbacks of technological progress."

Dr. Foster: "Exactly. Responsible innovation involves not only seeking advancements but also ensuring that these advancements contribute positively to society and the environment. It's about finding a balance between progress and sustainability."

Exhibit 4: Future Visions

The final exhibit Sarah visited was dedicated to visions of the future. It featured speculative technologies, environmental solutions, and societal changes projected for the coming decades. The space was filled with interactive models and virtual reality experiences that allowed visitors to explore potential futures.

Sarah: "The future is full of possibilities. How can we ensure that we're advancing in a way that's both innovative and responsible?"

Dr. Foster: "The future depends on the choices we make today. By focusing on incremental improvements and considering the long-term implications of our actions, we can shape a future that balances innovation with responsibility. It's about making thoughtful decisions and being proactive in addressing potential challenges."

Sarah participated in a VR simulation where she made decisions about future urban planning, technological development, and environmental sustainability. The simulation highlighted how her choices could influence the trajectory of future societies.

Sarah: "The VR simulation showed me how interconnected our decisions are. Each choice we make can significantly impact future generations. It's a powerful reminder of our responsibility to shape a positive future."

Dr. Foster: "Absolutely. Every individual's actions contribute to the broader mosaic of civilization. By making informed and thoughtful choices, we can help create a future that reflects our values and aspirations."

Reflecting on the Experience

As Sarah concluded her visit, she took a moment to reflect on her experiences. The museum had provided her with a comprehensive understanding of how civilization evolves and the role of individual actions in shaping the future.

Sarah: "This museum has given me a new perspective on the progression of civilization. It's clear that our advancements are built on the lessons of the past, and each of us has a part to play in shaping the future."

Dr. Foster: "I'm glad to hear that. The story of civilization is a mosaic, composed of countless individual contributions and decisions. By embracing innovation responsibly and learning from history, we can collectively create a better world."

Sarah left the museum feeling inspired and empowered. The immersive exhibits and interactive experiences had reinforced her understanding of how each person's actions contribute to the broader tapestry of human progress. The lessons learned from the past, combined with thoughtful decision-making in the present, could indeed shape a brighter future for all.

End of Chapter 3

In this chapter, Sarah's exploration of the interactive museum offers a detailed and immersive understanding of civilization's evolution. Through vibrant exhibits and interactive scenarios, she learns about the importance of balancing innovation with historical lessons and making thoughtful decisions to shape a positive future.

These haiku explore the evolution of civilization, the lessons from history, and the impact of individual choices on the future.

Chapter 3: Civilization's Mosaic - Free Verse Haiku

1. Timeless museum,
Ancient echoes come to life—
History unfolds.

2. Epochs dance in light,
From clay tablets to the stars—
Human progress sings.

3. Early footsteps trace,
Ancient tools and first writings—
Roots of our journey.

4. Renaissance art gleams,
Brushstrokes of a new vision—
Creativity blooms.

5. Innovation's spark,
Da Vinci's dreams take flight—
Future in the past.

6. Industrial hum,
Factories and steam engines—
Change's relentless beat.

7. Progress's dual face,
Advancement with costs revealed—
Balance is the key.

8. Interactive time,
History's whispers guide us—
Choices shape the path.

9. Silent clay tablets,
Stories etched in ancient lines—
Echoes of the past.

10. Innovation's forge,
From iron to silicon—
Mosaic of time.

11. Art and science blend,
Renaissance's legacy—
Wonder's vibrant hue.

12. Factories rise tall,
Steam and steel reshape the world—
Industry's dawn breaks.

13. Environmental cost,
As progress marches forward—
Lessons in the dust.

14. Virtual futures,
Visions of a new tomorrow—
Choices paint the path.

15. Ancient wisdom's voice,
Guides through the shifting sands—
History's compass.

16. Interactive screens,
Touch the past, embrace the now—
Time's woven fabric.

17. Renaissance rebirth,
Empirical light ignites—
Creativity soars.

18. Steam engines roar loud,
Changing lives with iron will—
Industry's grand march.

19. Mosaic of time,
Patterns of human progress—
Each thread tells a tale.

20. Future's bright mosaic,
Choices cast in virtual realms—
Shaping what's to come.

21. Ancient stone whispers,
History's soft, constant hum—
Echoes through the years.

22. Renaissance's blaze,
Art and science intertwine—
Innovation's spark.

23. Steam and steel collide,
Industrial dawn breaks through—
Change's fierce advance.

24. Interactive past,
Touch the threads of history—
Time's vast tapestry.

25. Lessons from the old,
Guide the steps of the present—
Future's path unfolds.

26. Clay and metal speak,
Foundations of our progress—
History's deep roots.

27. Artistry and thought,
Renaissance's vibrant burst—
Creativity reigns.

28. Factories and noise,
Steam engines drive the world's pulse—
Industry's great leap.

29. Vision's virtual,
Futures spun in simulated—
Choices cast in light.

30. Past's silent wisdom,
Shaping futures with each step—
Mosaic of change.

31. Renaissance dreamscapes,
Art and science forge ahead—
Creativity's call.

32. Iron, steam, and gears,
Industry's relentless drive—
Change's powerful roar.

33. Interactive space,
History's voice speaks anew—
Guiding our own course.

34. Ancient pathways laid,
Early steps in human quest—
Mosaic of time.

35. Renaissance sparks fire,
Empirical and divine—
Art and science blend.

36. Factories rise high,
Steam and steel reshape the world—
Industry's loud call.

37. Virtual futures,
Decisions in simulated—
Shaping what's ahead.

38. History's soft voice,
Guides through the ages' vast sea—
Ancient echoes speak.

39. Art's vivid rebirth,
Renaissance lights the dark sky—
Innovation's dawn.

40. Steam's thunderous roar,
Industry's pulse felt deep—
Progress marches on.

41. Interactive threads,
History's moments come alive—
Time's vibrant canvas.

42. Mosaic of years,
Each choice weaves into the next—
Future's tapestry.

43. Renaissance's light,
Art and intellect unite—
Creativity's fire.

44. Factories hum loud,
Iron and steam forge the path—
Industry's heartbeat.

45. Virtual visions,
Future's scenarios unfold—
Choices paint the way.

46. Ancient whispers call,
Guiding us through history's fog—
Lessons from the past.

47. Renaissance's burst,
Empirical dreams take flight—
Art and science merge.

48. Factories rise tall,
Steam engines drive the era—
Industry's great leap.

49. Futures in the screens,
Virtual worlds take their shape—
Shaping what will be.

50. History's soft hum,
Ancient echoes, modern dreams—
Mosaic of time.

51. Renaissance's blaze,
Art and thought collide and soar—
Creativity's spark.

52. Factories' loud roar,
Steam and steel reshape the world—
Progress's strong beat.

53. Interactive past,
Touch the threads of history—
Time's woven fabric.

54. Lessons from the past,
Guide us through the present's maze—
Future's path revealed.

55. Clay and metal speak,
Foundations of our progress—
History's deep roots.

56. Renaissance's fire,
Art and science forge ahead—
Innovation's dawn.

57. Steam's relentless drive,
Industry's pulse beats deep—
Change's powerful march.

58. Virtual realms spin,
Futures unfold in the light—
Choices cast their shape.

59. Ancient pathways traced,
Early steps in human quest—
Mosaic of years.

60. Renaissance rebirth,
Empirical light ignites—
Creativity blooms.

61. Factories and steam,
Industrial hums and roars—
Change's fierce advance.

62. Interactive time,
History's whispers guide us—
Choices shape the path.

63. Ancient wisdom calls,
Guiding through the shifting sands—
Echoes of the past.

64. Renaissance dreamscapes,
Art and science intertwine—
Innovation's spark.

65. Steam engines' loud pulse,
Industrial dawn breaks through—
Progress's great leap.

66. Virtual futures,
Decisions in simulations—
Shaping what's to come.

67. Mosaic of time,
Patterns of human progress—
Each thread tells a tale.

68. Ancient stone whispers,
History's soft, constant hum—
Echoes through the years.

69. Renaissance's blaze,
Art and science forge ahead—
Creativity's call.

70. Factories rise high,
Steam and steel reshape the world—
Industry's loud call.

71. Virtual scenarios,
Futures spun in simulated—
Choices cast in light.

72. History's soft voice,
Guides through the ages' vast sea—
Ancient echoes speak.

73. Art's vivid rebirth,
Renaissance lights the dark sky—
Innovation's dawn.

74. Steam's thunderous roar,
Industry's pulse felt deep—
Progress marches on.

75. Interactive space,
History's voice speaks anew—
Guiding our own course.

76. Ancient pathways laid,
Early steps in human quest—
Mosaic of time.

77. Renaissance sparks fire,
Empirical and divine—
Art and science blend.

78. Factories rise high,
Steam and steel reshape the world—
Industry's great leap.

79. Virtual futures,
Decisions in simulated—
Shaping what's ahead.

80. History's soft voice,
Guiding us through vast time's sea—
Ancient echoes call.

81. Art's vivid rebirth,
Renaissance lights the dark sky—
Creativity's dawn.

82. Steam's thunderous roar,
Industry's deep rhythm beats—
Progress marches forth.

83. Interactive past,
Touching threads of history—
Time's living tapestry.

84. Lessons from the old,
Shaping present and future—
Mosaic of change.

85. Clay and metal speak,
Foundations of progress rise—
Echoes from the past.

86. Renaissance's blaze,
Art and thought entwined in light—
Creativity's fire.

87. Factories hum loud,
Steam engines drive the world's pulse—
Industry's great leap.

88. Virtual futures,
Decisions cast in the light—
Shaping what will be.

89. Ancient whispers call,
Guiding us through history—
Lessons from the past.

90. Renaissance's spark,
Empirical dreams ignite—
Art and science merge.

91. Factories rise high,
Steam and steel transform the world—
Industry's loud roar.

92. Futures in the screens,
Virtual worlds taking shape—
Shaping what will come.

93. History's soft hum,
Ancient echoes guide us—
Mosaic of time.

94. Renaissance's light,
Art and intellect unite—
Innovation's dawn.

95. Steam's relentless drive,
Industry's rhythm beats strong—
Change's powerful march.

96. Interactive space,
Touch history's vibrant threads—
Time's vast fabric weaves.

97. Lessons from the past,
Guide present and future steps—
Mosaic of progress.

98. Clay and metal sing,
Foundations of progress laid—
History's deep roots.

99. Renaissance's fire,
Art and science push ahead—
Creativity blooms.

100. Factories rise tall,
Steam engines' relentless beat—
Industry's grand march.

101. Virtual futures,
Choices in the light unfold—
Shaping what's to come.

These haiku encapsulate the essence of Sarah's journey through the museum in Chapter 3, exploring the evolution of civilization, the lessons learned from history, and the profound impact of individual choices on shaping the future.

Chapter 4: The Labyrinth of Fear

Scene: The VR Labyrinth

Sarah's exploration of fear began in a state-of-the-art virtual reality lab. The room was dimly lit, filled with the soft hum of high-tech equipment and the faint glow of screens lining the walls. In the center stood a sleek VR headset on a pedestal, its surface shimmering under the lights. This was the gateway to the Labyrinth of Fear, a cutting-edge simulation designed to help individuals confront and overcome their deepest anxieties.

As Sarah approached the headset, her guide, Dr. Mia Reynolds, a psychologist specializing in anxiety and resilience training, greeted her warmly. Dr. Reynolds was known for her innovative approaches to mental health, and Sarah was eager to delve into the labyrinth under her guidance.

Dr. Reynolds: "Welcome, Sarah. Today, you'll be navigating a labyrinth designed to represent various fears and psychological barriers. Each turn you take will present you with different challenges and coping strategies. Are you ready to begin?"

Sarah: "Absolutely. I've read that facing fears directly can be transformative. I'm curious to see how this VR experience will help."

Dr. Reynolds: "That's the spirit. Remember, fear can be paralyzing, but confronting it is the first step towards overcoming it. Let's start by discussing some strategies that can help us deal with these fears."

Sarah nodded as she placed the VR headset over her eyes, the world around her dissolving into darkness before being replaced by the intricate, ever-shifting pathways of the labyrinth. The virtual environment was a complex network of corridors, each representing a different type of fear, from fear of failure to fear of the unknown.

Dr. Reynolds: "In this simulation, you'll encounter various scenarios designed to trigger different fears. As you navigate, consider using techniques such as mindfulness, cognitive restructuring, and gradual exposure. Understanding and addressing the root of your fears is crucial."

Sarah: "Got it. I'll keep those strategies in mind as I move through the labyrinth."

The labyrinth unfolded before Sarah in a series of elaborate, interconnected rooms and hallways, each designed to evoke a particular psychological challenge. The first room she entered was dimly lit, with shadows flickering on the walls, creating an atmosphere of eerie uncertainty.

Interactive Scene: The Shadow Room

Sarah's heart raced as she stepped into the room, the shadows seeming to twist and shift as if alive. Her fear of the unknown surged. She took a deep breath, recalling Dr. Reynolds' advice on mindfulness. She focused on her breathing, grounding herself in the present moment.

Sarah: (to herself) "I'm here now. I'm safe. These shadows are just a visual representation. I need to stay calm and assess the situation."

As Sarah walked further into the room, she encountered a series of shadows that seemed to whisper her deepest insecurities. The whispers grew louder, forming a cacophony of voices that echoed her fears of inadequacy and *failure. The walls seemed to close in, and the room felt increasingly claustrophobic.*

Dr. Reynolds (voice-over): *"Remember, Sarah, mindfulness is about being aware of your thoughts and feelings without letting them overwhelm you. Notice the shadows, but don't let them control you. Focus on your breath and your intention to move forward."*

Sarah closed her eyes for a moment, focusing on her breath. She visualized the shadows as harmless projections of her mind, rather than threats. Slowly, the whispers began to fade, and the shadows receded, revealing a door leading to the next room.

Sarah: *"I can do this. It's just a projection of my mind. I'm in control."*

Interactive Scene: The Failure Chamber

The next room was starkly different—a stark, clinical space filled with piles of crumpled papers and broken objects, symbolizing failure and rejection. Sarah's fear of failure loomed large as she looked around. The room seemed to pulse with a sense of despair and inadequacy.

Dr. Reynolds (voice-over): *"In this chamber, you'll face your fear of failure. Cognitive restructuring can help here. Challenge the negative thoughts and replace them with more balanced perspectives."*

Sarah approached a table where a large, flickering screen displayed a series of failed projects and rejected ideas. Her initial reaction was one of dread, but she remembered Dr. Reynolds' advice on cognitive restructuring. She began to question the validity of the negative thoughts.

Sarah: *"Failure isn't the end. It's a step in the learning process. Each failure teaches me something new and helps me grow."*

As Sarah repeated this affirmation, the failed projects on the screen began to transform into positive learning experiences. The broken objects on the floor turned into symbols of perseverance and growth. The room's oppressive atmosphere lightened, and a path leading to the next challenge opened up.

Sarah: *"Failure is just part of the journey. I can use it as a tool for improvement."*

Interactive Scene: The Social Anxiety Zone

Sarah entered the next room, which was filled with virtual people engaging in animated conversations. The room was designed to simulate social situations that might trigger social anxiety. Virtual individuals glanced at Sarah, their expressions shifting between curiosity and judgment.

Dr. Reynolds (voice-over): "This zone represents social anxiety. Gradual exposure is key here. Start by engaging with one virtual person at a time and practice positive self-talk."

Sarah took a deep breath and approached one of the virtual individuals, who greeted her with a friendly smile. The initial interaction was awkward, but Sarah reminded herself that the virtual scenario was designed for practice.

Sarah: "It's okay to feel nervous. I can take small steps and build my confidence."

With each interaction, Sarah felt her anxiety begin to diminish. The virtual people responded positively to her efforts, and the room's atmosphere shifted from one of discomfort to one of acceptance. Sarah felt a growing sense of accomplishment and ease.

Sarah: "I'm capable of handling social situations. I just need to take it one step at a time."

Interactive Scene: The Fear of the Unknown Chamber

The final room of the labyrinth was shrouded in complete darkness, with only faint, shifting lights offering glimpses of what lay ahead. The fear of the unknown was palpable, as the darkness seemed to stretch endlessly.

Dr. Reynolds (voice-over): "The fear of the unknown is often the most daunting. Embrace gradual exposure and mindfulness. Focus on the steps you're taking rather than the uncertainty."

Sarah hesitated for a moment before stepping into the darkness. She remembered that the path was a series of small, manageable steps rather than a single leap into the void. She took one step forward, then another, each time feeling a bit more confident as her eyes adjusted to the darkness.

Sarah: "I don't need to see the entire path to move forward. I can take it step by step."

Gradually, the darkness began to recede, revealing a path illuminated by soft, reassuring light. Sarah navigated through the remaining portion of the labyrinth with growing confidence, each step reinforcing her ability to manage uncertainty.

Sarah: "Facing the unknown doesn't have to be overwhelming. I can handle it by focusing on each step."

Conclusion of the Labyrinth

As Sarah emerged from the labyrinth, she removed the VR headset, feeling a sense of accomplishment and newfound clarity. Dr. Reynolds awaited her, a supportive smile on her face.

Dr. Reynolds: "How was the experience, Sarah? Did you find the strategies helpful?"

Sarah: "It was incredibly insightful. Confronting each fear and using the strategies really helped me understand how to manage my anxieties. Mindfulness, cognitive restructuring, and gradual exposure are powerful tools."

Dr. Reynolds: "I'm glad to hear that. Remember, the labyrinth is a representation of internal challenges. The skills you practiced here can be applied to real-life situations. Facing fears is a continuous journey, but with these strategies, you're better equipped to navigate them."

Sarah: "I feel more prepared to handle my fears now. It's empowering to realize that I have the tools to manage anxiety and build resilience."

Dr. Reynolds: "That's wonderful to hear. Embracing your fears and using effective coping strategies is a significant step toward personal growth. Keep practicing these techniques, and you'll continue to build confidence and resilience."

As Sarah left the lab, she felt a renewed sense of empowerment. The labyrinth had provided her with practical tools and valuable insights into managing her fears. She was ready to face her anxieties with greater confidence, knowing that she had the strategies to navigate the complexities of her psychological barriers.

End of Chapter 4

In this chapter, Sarah's journey through the Labyrinth of Fear provides a deep exploration of confronting psychological barriers and developing coping strategies. Through interactive VR experiences, she encounters various fears, employing mindfulness, cognitive restructuring, and gradual exposure to manage her anxieties. The chapter underscores the importance *of facing fears directly and utilizing practical tools to build resilience and confidence.*

These haiku explore the different aspects of confronting and overcoming fears, using VR simulations and psychological techniques.

---

1. VR labyrinth,
Shadows twist and fears take shape—
Confronting the dark.

2. Fear's phantom shadows,
Dancing on the labyrinth—
Courage meets the night.

3. Breath in the darkness,
Mindfulness the guiding light—
Shadows lose their grip.

4. Crumpled dreams on floors,
Failure's weight heavy and cold—
Rise from broken hopes.

5. Echoes of defeat,
Fading as new thoughts arise—
Failures forge the path.

6. Social faces stare,
Anxiety's silent gaze—
Steps through virtual crowds.

7. Gradual exposure,
Each small step builds confidence—
Social fears dissolve.

8. Unknown darkness waits,
Steps uncertain, heartbeats quick—
Embrace the journey.

9. Fear's labyrinth vast,
Paths of anxiety and doubt—
Courage lights the way.

10. Shadows whisper loud,
Heart races in eerie gloom—
Mindfulness holds firm.

11. *Failed projects scattered,*
Lessons lie within the mess—
Growth from shattered dreams.

12. *Voices of the past,*
Tales of failure, harsh and cold—
New thoughts rewrite paths.

13. *Virtual faces,*
Judgment in the crowd's soft hum—
Confidence steps through.

14. *Social maze unwinds,*
Gradual steps through chatter's fog—
Confidence takes hold.

15. *Unknown stretches wide,*
Darkness swallows the pathway—
Step by step reveals.

16. *Mindfulness in dark,*
Breath anchors through fear's embrace—
Shadows lose their sting.

17. *Failure's cluttered room,*
Broken dreams and crumpled hopes—
Resilience emerges.

18. *Anxiety's crowd,*
Faces turn in silent judgment—
Small steps build courage.

19. *Fear of the dark paths,*
Steps taken in soft, cautious light—
Bravery unfolds.

20. *VR labyrinth,*
Confronting fears in digital—
Strength in virtual.

21. *Shadows' whispers fade,*
Mindfulness brings light to fears—
Darkness softens now.

22. *Failure's harsh echoes,*
Broken dreams scattered on ground—
Lessons rise anew.

23. Social anxieties,
Virtual faces watch and judge—
Confidence steps through.

24. Unknown stretches long,
Steps illuminate the dark—
Bravery leads on.

25. Breath in shadows deep,
Mindfulness guides through the fear—
Darkness yields to light.

26. Crumpled hopes on floor,
Failure's lessons etched in time—
Growth from shattered dreams.

27. Crowd of anxious faces,
Virtual eyes watch and weigh—
Confidence prevails.

28. Dark paths beckon close,
Steps brave through the unknown fears—
Journey lights the way.

29. Mindfulness holds fast,
Breathing through the fearsome dark—
Shadows start to fade.

30. Room of broken dreams,
Failure's mess, a teacher's voice—
Resilience is born.

31. Social maze of doubt,
Virtual faces gaze stern—
Small steps forge new paths.

32. Unknown darkness calls,
Each step through the murk reveals—
Courage lights the way.

33. Fear's whispering shade,
Breath anchors in shifting dark—
Calm amidst the storm.

34. Failure's scattered past,
Lessons from each broken piece—
Hope rises again.

35. Social fears abate,
Gradual steps through virtual—
Confidence blooms forth.

36. Dark unknown awaits,
Steps through the mist lead to light—
Bravery unveils.

37. Shadows lost their grip,
Mindfulness a guiding star—
Darkness starts to wane.

38. Failed hopes on the floor,
Lessons in the crumpled past—
New strength from the fall.

39. Social anxieties,
Virtual eyes watch and weigh—
Confidence ignites.

40. Path of fear unknown,
Steps forward through murky dark—
Courage lights the path.

41. Mindfulness prevails,
Breath steady through fearful night—
Shadows start to fade.

42. Failure's cluttered room,
Lessons buried in the dust—
Resilience now grows.

43. Social faces judge,
Virtual crowd's silent gaze—
Confidence steps forth.

44. Unknown paths unravel,
Steps in dark lead to the light—
Courage guides the way.

45. Fear's shadows retreat,
Breath anchors in calm resolve—
Darkness fades away.

46. Crumpled dreams on ground,
Failure's harsh lessons taught well—
New hopes rise from the dust.

47. Social anxiety,
Virtual faces and gaze—
Confidence emerges.

48. Unknown stretches long,
Step by step through darkened paths—
Bravery reveals.

49. Shadows in the dark,
Mindfulness guides through the fear—
Calm replaces dread.

50. Failure's mess on floor,
Lessons in the broken dreams—
Strength forged from the fall.

51. Social crowd of doubt,
Virtual faces judge hard—
Confidence builds strong.

52. Dark paths open wide,
Each step forward reveals light—
Courage conquers fear.

53. Mindfulness holds fast,
Breath steady through the unknown—
Shadows start to fade.

54. Failure's scattered past,
Lessons in each crumpled piece—
Growth from the lessons.

55. Social fears dissolve,
Virtual faces lose weight—
Confidence shines bright.

56. Unknown path ahead,
Step by step through darkest night—
Bravery unfolds.

57. Fear's shadows retreat,
Mindfulness a guiding force—
Darkness softens now.

58. Failed dreams on the floor,
Lessons from each broken shard—
Resilience takes root.

59. Social doubts fade fast,
Virtual gaze loses weight—
Confidence prevails.

60. Dark paths beckon close,
Each step through the fog reveals—
Courage lights the way.

61. Mindfulness remains,
Breath steady through fear's dark veil—
Shadows start to yield.

62. Failure's harsh echoes,
Broken dreams and lessons learned—
Strength from the fragments.

63. Social anxieties,
Virtual eyes weigh and judge—
Confidence prevails.

64. Unknown stretches wide,
Each step through dark reveals light—
Bravery unfolds.

65. Shadows lose their edge,
Mindfulness guides through the night—
Darkness fades away.

66. Crumpled hopes lie still,
Failure's mess a teacher's tool—
New hope rises up.

67. Virtual faces,
Social fears and judgments—
Confidence builds strong.

68. Dark paths open wide,
Steps through the unknown reveal—
Courage lights the way.

69. Mindfulness holds firm,
Breathing through the fearsome dark—
Shadows start to fade.

70. Failure's cluttered ground,
Lessons from the broken past—
Resilience grows strong.

71. Social anxieties,
Virtual gazes weigh—
Confidence emerges.

72. Unknown darkness calls,
Each step forward reveals light—
Courage shines through fear.

73. Fear's shadows recede,
Mindfulness a steady guide—
Darkness yields to calm.

74. Crumpled dreams on floor,
Failure's harsh lessons guide—
Strength emerges bright.

75. Social doubts dissolve,
Virtual faces lose weight—
Confidence shines clear.

76. Dark paths stretch ahead,
Each step through the murk reveals—
Courage leads the way.

77. Mindfulness remains,
Breath steady through darkest fears—
Shadows fade away.

78. Failure's scattered past,
Lessons in each crumpled shard—
Strength rises anew.

79. Social anxieties,
Virtual eyes watch and weigh—
Confidence prevails.

80. Unknown stretches long,
Each step reveals hidden light—
Bravery unfolds.

81. Shadows lose their edge,
Mindfulness guides through the dark—
Calm amidst the fear.

82. Failed hopes lie still,
Lessons from the broken dreams—
Resilience grows strong.

83. Social doubts dissolve,
Virtual faces lose weight—
Confidence builds bright.

84. Dark paths open wide,
Each step through the dark reveals—
Courage lights the path.

85. Mindfulness holds fast,
Breath steady through fearsome night—
Shadows start to wane.

86. Failure's cluttered room,
Lessons from each broken piece—
Strength forged anew.

87. Social anxieties,
Virtual gazes weigh hard—
Confidence prevails.

88. Unknown stretches long,
Steps through dark reveal the light—
Bravery takes flight.

89. Shadows lose their grip,
Mindfulness the guiding star—
Darkness starts to fade.

90. Crumpled dreams on ground,
Lessons in the failures shared—
Hope rises again.

91. Social crowd of doubt,
Virtual faces judge stern—
Confidence steps through.

92. Dark paths call ahead,
Each step through the fog reveals—
Courage lights the way.

93. Mindfulness prevails,
Breath steady through the dark fears—
Shadows yield to calm.

94. Failure's scattered past,
Lessons from the broken dreams—
Strength from the fall.

95. Social fears abate,
Virtual faces lose weight—
Confidence blooms forth.

96. Unknown stretches wide,
Each step forward reveals light—
Bravery unfolds.

97. Shadows recede fast,
Mindfulness guides through the dark—
Darkness fades away.

98. Crumpled hopes lie still,
Lessons in the shattered past—
New strength from the fall.

99. Social doubts dissolve,
Virtual faces lose weight—
Confidence prevails.

100. Dark paths stretch ahead,
Steps through the unknown reveal—
Courage lights the way.

101. Mindfulness holds firm,
Breathing through the fearsome dark—
Shadows start to fade.

These haikus explore the emotional landscape of confronting fears, navigating psychological challenges, and using various strategies to build resilience and courage. Each haiku is designed to capture the essence of Sarah's journey through the VR labyrinth in Chapter 4.

Chapter 6: Khudrat (The Nature)

Sarah's journey into the eco-simulation was a departure from the high-tech, fear-confronting realms she had previously explored. This time, she was stepping into a virtual world designed to mirror the delicate balance of nature and the impact of human activity. The room she entered was transformed into a lush, digital landscape, complete with vibrant forests, flowing rivers, and diverse ecosystems. It was an immersive experience that promised to deepen her understanding of environmental stewardship.

Setting the Scene

The simulation was a marvel of technology and nature intertwined. The air was filled with the scent of fresh pine and the sound of birds chirping. The vibrant colors of the digital flora and fauna were remarkably lifelike, creating a serene yet dynamic environment. Sarah could almost feel the virtual breeze on her face as she walked through the forest, the ground beneath her feet soft and yielding.

Standing beside her was Dr. Anil Patel, an eco-expert renowned for his work in sustainable development and environmental science. He was there to guide Sarah through the simulation and help her grasp the critical importance of integrating technology and nature.

Dr. Patel: "Welcome to the eco-simulation, Sarah. This is a digital representation of various ecosystems and the impact of human activities on them. Today, we'll explore how advancements can be aligned with environmental stewardship."

Sarah: "It's incredible to see nature in such detail. How can we ensure that our technological advancements don't negatively impact the environment?"

Dr. Patel: "That's a crucial question. The key lies in integrating sustainable practices and respecting natural processes. Even small changes, like reducing waste, conserving resources, and adopting eco-friendly technologies, can lead to significant improvements."

Sarah began her exploration in a lush forest ecosystem. The simulation allowed her to interact with various elements of the environment—plants, animals, and water systems. Each interaction was designed to demonstrate the delicate balance of nature and the potential consequences of human actions.

Exploration and Interactions

1. The Forest Ecosystem

Sarah's first stop was a thriving forest, filled with tall trees, diverse plant life, and a rich tapestry of animal sounds. She approached a virtual river flowing gently through the forest, noticing how it supported various forms of life. The simulation offered interactive options to observe how different factors, such as pollution or deforestation, affected the river and its surroundings.

Sarah: "I see that the river is clear and full of life right now. What happens if we introduce pollutants or cut down trees?"

Dr. Patel: "Let's find out. We'll start by introducing a small amount of virtual pollutants into the river and observe the effects."

Sarah interacted with a control panel, introducing simulated pollutants into the river. Almost immediately, the water began to change color, and the once-clear stream was clouded by the pollutants. The virtual fish and plants started to show signs of distress—fish floating lethargically and plants wilting.

Dr. Patel: "As you can see, pollution has a dramatic impact on aquatic life. The ecosystem becomes unbalanced, affecting everything from the smallest microorganisms to the larger animals dependent on the river."

Sarah: "It's astonishing how quickly things can go wrong. What can be done to reverse or prevent this kind of damage?"

Dr. Patel: "Preventative measures are key. Reducing pollution at the source, using sustainable agricultural practices, and implementing effective waste management systems can all help maintain the health of our waterways."

Sarah engaged in a task to clean the river using virtual tools. As she removed the pollutants, the water gradually cleared, and the aquatic life began to recover. This exercise highlighted the potential for restoration and the importance of proactive environmental management.

2. The Urban Environment

Next, Sarah was transported to a virtual urban environment, where she observed a bustling city with high-rise buildings, busy streets, and industrial areas. The simulation provided insights into how urban development impacts the environment, including air quality, energy consumption, and waste production.

Sarah: "In urban areas, how can we balance development with environmental conservation?"

Dr. Patel: "Urban areas present unique challenges, but there are many strategies to make them more sustainable. Green building practices, energy-efficient technologies, and waste reduction are crucial. Let's explore some of these solutions."

Sarah interacted with the urban simulation, exploring features like green roofs, solar panels, and waste recycling systems. She observed how these sustainable practices could mitigate the negative impacts of urbanization.

Dr. Patel: "Notice how the integration of green spaces and renewable energy sources reduces the city's carbon footprint and improves air quality. It's about finding harmony between development and nature."

Sarah: "It's impressive to see how technology can support sustainability in urban settings. What about waste management?"

Dr. Patel: "Effective waste management involves reducing waste generation, recycling materials, and composting organic waste. In the simulation, you can set up recycling stations and observe their impact on the environment."

Sarah set up virtual recycling stations and composting systems throughout the city. The simulation demonstrated how these practices reduced landfill waste and supported a circular economy, where materials were reused and recycled.

3. The Agricultural Zone

Sarah's final stop was a virtual agricultural zone, where she explored sustainable farming practices. The simulation showcased various farming techniques, including traditional methods, organic farming, and modern agro-tech solutions.

Sarah: "How do different farming practices affect the environment?"

Dr. Patel: "Agriculture can have a significant impact on the environment, depending on the practices used. Traditional farming methods might lead to soil degradation, while organic farming and agro-tech solutions can promote soil health and reduce chemical use."

Sarah interacted with different farming setups, observing the effects on soil quality, water usage, and biodiversity. She compared traditional farming, which led to soil erosion and reduced fertility, with organic farming and agro-tech solutions, which promoted soil health and efficient resource use.

Dr. Patel: "Sustainable farming practices, such as crop rotation, organic fertilizers, and efficient water management, help maintain soil health and reduce environmental impact. This zone demonstrates the potential for agriculture to support environmental sustainability."

Sarah: "It's fascinating to see how farming techniques can either harm or help the environment. What can individuals do to support sustainable agriculture?"

Dr. Patel: "Individuals can support sustainable agriculture by choosing locally-sourced and organic products, reducing food waste, and supporting farmers who use eco-friendly practices. Every choice contributes to a healthier planet."

Reflections and Insights

As Sarah concluded her exploration, she reflected on the interconnectedness of nature and human activity. The eco-simulation had provided her with a deeper understanding of how technological and societal advancements could align with environmental stewardship. The interactive experiences highlighted the importance of integrating sustainable practices and respecting natural processes.

Sarah: "This simulation has shown me the profound impact of our actions on the environment. Even small changes, like reducing waste or conserving resources, can make a significant difference."

Dr. Patel: "Exactly. Our goal is to promote a harmonious relationship between technology, society, and nature. Every action counts, and by adopting sustainable practices, we can create a better future for ourselves and the planet."

Sarah left the eco-simulation with a renewed sense of purpose. She understood that the journey toward environmental stewardship was not only about technological innovation but also about making conscious choices that respected and preserved the natural world. The experience reinforced the idea that every action—no matter how small—could contribute to a more sustainable and balanced future.

End of Chapter 6

In this chapter, Sarah's exploration of the eco-simulation provided a comprehensive understanding of how human activities impact the environment and the importance of integrating sustainable practices. Through interactive experiences in various ecosystems, urban settings, and agricultural zones, Sarah learned about the interconnectedness of nature and technology. The chapter emphasized the significance of environmental stewardship and the potential for every individual's actions to contribute to a healthier planet.

Chapter 7: The Journey of Mastery

Sarah entered the skill-building center with a mix of excitement and apprehension. The environment was designed to simulate a series of real-world challenges that required not just skill but also perseverance, patience, and strategic problem-solving. This chapter marked a crucial turning point in her journey, focusing on the importance of dedication and the pitfalls of seeking shortcuts.

Setting the Scene

The skill-building center was a futuristic yet inviting space, filled with various interactive modules. Each module represented a different challenge or skill set—ranging from complex problem-solving scenarios to creative tasks that required a blend of cognitive and manual skills. The environment was both inspiring and challenging, designed to push participants to their limits and beyond.

Sarah was greeted by her mentor for this journey, Dr. Rebecca Lewis, a renowned expert in mastery and skill development. Dr. Lewis was known for her research on the role of perseverance in achieving excellence and was eager to guide Sarah through this transformative experience.

Dr. Lewis: "Welcome, Sarah. Today, you'll be navigating through a series of interactive modules designed to test your patience, strategic thinking, and dedication. Mastery is not about quick wins but about sustained effort and continuous learning."

Sarah: "I've heard that patience is key to achieving mastery, but I've always wondered why it's so important. Can you explain?"

Dr. Lewis: "Certainly. Mastery requires more than just innate talent; it demands dedication and time. Quick fixes may offer temporary results, but true excellence is achieved through persistent effort, learning from failures, and continuously refining your skills."

With this introduction, Sarah began her journey through the skill-building modules, each of which provided a unique challenge that tested her ability to stay focused and persistent.

1. The Puzzle of Patience

Sarah's first module was a complex puzzle challenge. The puzzle was not just a simple jigsaw but a multi-layered enigma requiring a series of logical steps to solve. The challenge simulated a real-world problem that required attention to detail, patience, and systematic thinking.

As Sarah worked on the puzzle, she encountered numerous setbacks. Pieces seemed to fit in the wrong places, and her progress felt painstakingly slow. Frustration began to creep in, but Sarah remembered Dr. Lewis's advice about the importance of patience.

Sarah: "This puzzle is taking so long! It feels like I'm making no progress at all."

Dr. Lewis: "Remember, Sarah, mastery is about persistence. Each small step you take, each mistake you make, is part of the learning process. Patience will help you see the bigger picture."

Sarah took a deep breath and refocused her efforts. She began to approach the puzzle with renewed determination, taking the time to analyze each piece and how it fit into the larger design. Slowly but surely, her persistence paid off. The puzzle started to come together, and Sarah felt a deep sense of accomplishment as she completed it.

2. The Creative Challenge

The next module was a creative challenge that required Sarah to design a product from scratch. She had to conceptualize, plan, and then build a prototype using virtual tools. The task was designed to test not only her creativity but also her ability to deal with the iterative nature of the creative process.

Sarah began by brainstorming ideas and sketching designs. The process was full of trial and error—ideas that seemed promising at first often needed to be revised or scrapped entirely. Each iteration brought new insights and challenges.

Sarah: "I keep running into problems with my design. Every time I think I'm close to the final product, something goes wrong."

Dr. Lewis: "Creativity is an iterative process. Each failure is an opportunity to learn and refine your approach. Patience in this process allows you to understand what works and what doesn't, leading to a more refined and successful outcome."

Sarah took this advice to heart. She embraced the iterative process, making adjustments and improvements based on her observations and feedback. Her final prototype was a testament to her patience and perseverance, illustrating how disciplined practice leads to mastery in creative endeavors.

3. The Strategic Game

The third module was a strategic game that simulated real-world business scenarios. Sarah was tasked with managing a virtual company, making decisions on production, marketing, and finance. The game required strategic thinking and long-term planning, emphasizing the importance of patience in achieving sustained success.

Sarah faced numerous challenges, including fluctuating market conditions and competition from other virtual companies. Each decision she made had consequences, and the game required careful planning and adaptation.

Sarah: "It's challenging to keep up with all the variables and make the right decisions. It feels like the stakes are so high."

Dr. Lewis: "In strategic planning, patience is crucial. You need to balance short-term gains with long-term goals. Each decision should be made with careful consideration of its potential impact over time."

Sarah adopted a patient and strategic approach, making decisions based on thorough analysis and long-term goals rather than immediate results. Her virtual company gradually grew and succeeded, demonstrating how patience and strategic thinking are essential for achieving mastery in business and management.

4. The Problem-Solving Maze

The final module was a problem-solving maze designed to test Sarah's ability to navigate complex scenarios and find solutions. The maze was filled with obstacles, puzzles, and challenges that required creative problem-solving and perseverance.

As Sarah worked her way through the maze, she encountered various obstacles that tested her resolve. Some paths led to dead ends, while others presented unexpected challenges. It was a true test of her ability to stay focused and persistent.

Sarah: *"This maze is incredibly complex. I keep hitting dead ends and facing new challenges."*

Dr. Lewis: *"Every obstacle is an opportunity to learn and adapt. Patience allows you to approach each problem with a clear mind and find innovative solutions. Mastery involves navigating these complexities with perseverance and resilience."*

Sarah approached each obstacle with a problem-solving mindset, using her previous experiences and insights to find her way through the maze. Her determination and patience paid off as she successfully navigated the maze and reached the final goal.

Reflections and Insights

As Sarah completed the final module, she reflected on her journey through the skill-building center. The challenges had tested her patience, creativity, strategic thinking, and problem-solving abilities. Through each module, she had experienced firsthand the importance of sustained effort and the pitfalls of seeking shortcuts.

Sarah: *"This journey has been eye-opening. I've learned that true mastery requires not just skill but also a commitment to the process. Patience and perseverance are key."*

Dr. Lewis: *"Absolutely. Mastery is not achieved through quick fixes but through consistent effort, learning from failures, and continually refining your skills. The rewards come from the dedication you put into the process."*

Sarah left the skill-building center with a renewed sense of purpose and commitment. She understood that achieving mastery was a journey of continuous learning and improvement, not a destination marked by instant success. The experiences in the interactive modules had reinforced the value of perseverance and the importance of approaching her goals with patience and dedication.

End of Chapter 7

In this chapter, Sarah's journey through the skill-building modules highlighted the critical role of patience and perseverance in achieving mastery. The interactive challenges emphasized the value of consistent effort, strategic problem-solving, and disciplined practice. Sarah's experience underscored the idea that true excellence comes from sustained dedication and learning from failures, inspiring her to approach her goals with renewed commitment and determination.

focusing on the themes of perseverance, patience, and the journey toward mastery:

---

1. **Puzzle pieces fit,**
Silent patience mends the gaps—
Victory unfolds.

2. **Time's slow progress shows,**
Details emerge, work revealed—
Mastery takes shape.

3. **Frustration's sharp edge,**
Softened by a steady hand—
Focus carves the path.

4. **Each step builds the bridge,**
Through the maze of trial and time—
Patience finds its way.

5. **Drafts of creation,**
Failure sketches out success—
Artistry evolves.

6. **Quiet persistence,**
Crafting dreams from fragments lost—
Strength in each setback.

7. **Puzzle in pieces,**
Every misfit teaches more—
Completeness unfolds.

8. **Creative process,**
Iterations blend and shift—
Art takes time to birth.

9. **Game of strategy,**
Moves laid out, paths intertwine—
Patience plays its hand.

10. **Thoughtful decisions,**
Shape the future's complex web—
Mastery's quiet.

11. **Obstacles arise,**
Each a test of will and grit—
Resolve finds the way.

12. **Lost in complex maze,**
Every turn and challenge shows—
Victory in sight.

13. **Strategic patience,**
Plans evolve, futures unfold—
Success is nurtured.

14. **Steps through darkened paths,**
Learning shadows guide the way—
Courage lights the dawn.

15. **Puzzles are pieces,**
Each moment builds the whole scene—
Mastery in time.

16. **Sketches turn to form,**
Creation's slow rhythm beats—
Art is born in waits.

17. **Game's endless trials,**
Victory through perseverance—
Strategy unfolds.

18. **Through failures we grow,**
Lessons learned in each attempt—
Strength in every fall.

19. **Maze of endless turns,**
Pathways twist, but patience sees—
The end is revealed.

20. **Design's intricate,**
Failures shape the final view—
Perseverance wins.

21. **Strategic choices,**
Plan and adapt with each move—
Mastery in play.

22. **Building from the start,**
Every mistake builds the path—
Success through effort.

23. **Each piece slowly fits,**
Puzzle's patience proves its worth—
Complete with calm hands.

24. **Art in slow progress,**
Iterations refine skill—
Mastery is time.

25. **Maze's twisting paths,**
Challenge and patience converge—
End in sight reveals.

26. **Strategic foresight,**
Plan and act with steady hands—
Mastery in time.

27. **Creativity,**
Crafted through iterative—
Artistry is born.

28. **Complex decisions,**
Patience guides through twists and turns—
Victory achieved.

29. **Puzzle's patience grows,**
Each piece fits with careful hands—
Completion in sight.

30. **Creative process,**
Drafts refine to final form—
Art in evolution.

31. **Strategic patience,**
Decisions shape the outcome—
Mastery unfolds.

32. **Endless maze of paths,**
Every turn reveals a clue—
Perseverance wins.

33. **Trial shapes the skill,**
Failures teach the path to take—
Mastery is growth.

34. **Puzzle pieces blend,**
Each attempt builds the whole view—
Victory is earned.

35. **Art's slow progress shows,**
Creative patience in play—
Final work revealed.

36. **Game's complex layers,**
Strategy meets patience here—
Mastery achieved.

37. **Steps through winding maze,**
Challenges guide, resolve grows—
Victory unfolds.

38. **Creation's rhythm,**
Drafts evolve through persistence—
Artistry emerges.

39. **Strategic thinking,**
Patience shapes the final path—
Success through foresight.

40. **Every piece a test,**
Puzzle's patience builds the scene—
Completion is near.

41. **Creative patience,**
Each revision refines skill—
Mastery in time.

42. **Maze of trials twists,**
Navigating through each turn—
Victory awaits.

43. **Strategic patience,**
Decisions craft the outcome—
Mastery in wait.

44. **Art's evolution,**
Drafts and revisions shape it—
Final work revealed.

45. **Puzzle pieces join,**
Patience crafts the final form—
Completion in time.

46. **Every move a step,**
Game's strategy builds success—
Patience plays its part.

47. **Obstacles challenge,**
Each a lesson learned in time—
Strength through persistence.

48. **Creative drafts show,**
Iterations refine work—
Mastery takes form.

49. **Maze of endless paths,**
Patience and resolve unite—
Victory is close.

50. **Puzzle's patience shows,**
Each piece fits with careful hand—
Completion revealed.

51. **Creative journey,**
Drafts and mistakes shape the path—
Artistry refined.

52. **Strategic foresight,**
Every move a step toward—
Mastery in time.

53. **Through the maze of doubt,**
Each turn reveals a new clue—
Victory in wait.

54. **Puzzle pieces fit,**
Patience builds the whole design—
Victory unfolds.

55. **Art's iterative,**
Each draft shapes the final form—
Mastery through time.

56. **Game's endless challenges,**
Strategic patience reveals—
Success through each play.

57. Complex paths emerge,
Each obstacle shapes the path—
Perseverance wins.

58. Puzzle in progress,
Every piece adds to the whole—
Completion in sight.

59. Creative process,
Iterations refine work—
Artistry takes shape.

60. Maze of twists and turns,
Patience guides through every step—
Victory reveals.

61. Strategic planning,
Every move builds the outcome—
Mastery achieved.

62. Puzzle's patience shows,
Each piece fits with careful thought—
Completion in time.

63. Creative drafts lead,
Through revisions and trials—
Artistry refined.

64. Game's strategic play,
Patience and skill craft success—
Mastery through time.

65. Maze's path reveals,
Each challenge a lesson learned—
Victory in sight.

66. Puzzle pieces blend,
Each attempt builds the final view—
Success through patience.

67. Creative journey,
Drafts and errors shape the work—
Mastery is time.

68. Strategic moves show,
Patience in each decision—
Success through foresight.

69. Obstacles teach strength,
Each challenge refines the path—
Victory is earned.

70. Puzzle's patience builds,
Every piece fits with purpose—
Completion in sight.

71. Creative drafts grow,
Revisions shape the final—
Mastery through time.

72. Game's endless trials,
Strategic patience reveals—
Success through each play.

73. Maze of paths and turns,
Each challenge a test of will—
Victory unfolds.

74. Puzzle's patience grows,
Each piece adds to the whole view—
Completion achieved.

75. Creative process,
Iterations shape the art—
Mastery takes form.

76. Strategic thinking,
Each move builds the final path—
Success through foresight.

77. Obstacles refine,
Each challenge strengthens resolve—
Victory is near.

78. Puzzle pieces fit,
Patience crafts the final view—
Completion revealed.

79. Creative drafts lead,
Revisions shape the artwork—
Mastery in time.

80. Game's strategic play,
Patience and skill build success—
Mastery achieved.

81. Maze's path reveals,
Each challenge guides the journey—
Victory in sight.

82. Puzzle's patience shows,
Every piece fits with intent—
Completion in time.

83. Creative drafts evolve,
Revisions refine the form—
Mastery is growth.

84. Strategic foresight,
Each decision shapes the end—
Success through patience.

85. Obstacles teach lessons,
Each challenge builds the path ahead—
Victory unfolds.

86. Puzzle's patience builds,
Every piece fits with care—
Completion in sight.

87. Creative journey,
Drafts and errors shape the work—
Artistry refined.

88. Game's strategic moves,
Patience and skill craft success—
Mastery through time.

89. Maze of twists and turns,
Each challenge a lesson learned—
Victory in sight.

90. Puzzle's patience shows,
Each piece fits into the whole—
Completion revealed.

91. Creative drafts grow,
Revisions shape the final—
Mastery in time.

92. Strategic planning,
Each move builds the final path—
Success through foresight.

93. **Obstacles refine,**
Each challenge strengthens resolve—
Victory is near.

94. **Puzzle pieces join,**
Patience crafts the final form—
Completion in sight.

95. **Creative drafts lead,**
Through revisions and trials—
Mastery takes shape.

96. **Game's endless challenges,**
Patience and strategy win—
Success achieved here.

97. **Maze of endless paths,**
Each turn reveals a new clue—
Victory unfolds.

98. **Puzzle's patience builds,**
Every piece adds to the view—
Completion revealed.

99. **Creative journey,**
Drafts and mistakes shape the path—
Mastery in time.

100. **Strategic moves show,**
Patience builds the final outcome—
Mastery is earned.

101. **Maze's challenges,**
Each twist and turn teaches more—
Victory is close.

These haikus capture the essence of perseverance, patience, and the journey towards mastery explored in Chapter 7. Each poem reflects the incremental progress and strategic approach necessary to achieve success and mastery.

Epilogue: A Harmonious Future

As Sarah concluded her journey through the multifaceted worlds of village life, technology, civilization, and personal growth, she found herself reflecting on the profound insights gained from her experiences. Her adventures had not only shaped her understanding of each distinct domain but also illustrated their interconnectedness in creating a more harmonious and fulfilling world. The novel's interactive and immersive elements had provided her—and by extension, the readers—with a holistic view of how individual actions and societal advancements intertwine to foster a balanced future.

The Culmination of Insights

Sarah's travels began in the peaceful village, where she had observed the beauty of simplicity and the profound impact of community on individual well-being. This experience had grounded her understanding of the human need for connection, stability, and the psychological benefits of a life lived in harmony with nature. The village life had taught her that fulfillment often comes from embracing simplicity and nurturing relationships, values that would later inform her approach to the more complex challenges of technology and civilization.

Her journey continued into the realm of artificial intelligence, where Dr. Liam's insights illuminated the parallels between AI learning processes and human development. Sarah learned that while AI adapts through patterns and data, humans, too, benefit from breaking tasks into manageable steps, learning from feedback, and iterative progress. This experience underscored the importance of structured approaches and persistence, applicable not only in technological advancements but also in personal growth.

The interactive museum of civilization had been another eye-opener. Moving through different epochs, Sarah saw how incremental advancements and thoughtful changes shaped the course of human history. The curator's advice about balancing innovation with respect for past lessons resonated deeply with her. Sarah understood that contributing to civilization responsibly involved integrating new ideas with an awareness of historical context, ensuring that progress did not come at the expense of foundational values.

In the labyrinth of fear, Sarah confronted her own psychological barriers. The VR experience had exposed her to various fears and coping strategies, providing practical tools for managing anxiety and building resilience. This journey through the labyrinth illustrated that overcoming fear is a gradual *process, one that requires patience and self-awareness. The experience highlighted that addressing fears is crucial for personal development and achieving a sense of inner peace.*

The eco-simulation had been a powerful reminder of the importance of aligning technological and societal progress with environmental stewardship. Sarah interacted with virtual ecosystems and experimented with sustainable practices, learning that even small, thoughtful changes can lead to significant improvements in environmental health. The eco-expert's guidance about integrating sustainable practices reinforced the idea that every action, no matter how minor, contributes to the broader goal of preserving and enhancing the natural world.

Finally, Sarah's venture into the skill-building modules demonstrated the value of perseverance and patience in achieving mastery. Each challenge—from the complex puzzle to the creative design and strategic game—emphasized that mastery is a journey marked by consistent effort, learning from failures, and avoiding shortcuts. Sarah's experience illustrated that true excellence is achieved through dedication and a willingness to embrace the iterative nature of skill development.

A Vision for the Future

As Sarah reflected on her journey, she envisioned a future where the principles she had learned could be applied to create a more harmonious and fulfilling world. Her experiences had shown her that personal growth, technological advancement, and societal progress are deeply interconnected, and that contributing to a better future requires a holistic approach.

1. Integrating Simplicity and Connection:

Sarah's time in the village had demonstrated the profound impact of simplicity and community on individual well-being. In a rapidly changing world, maintaining these values can provide a stabilizing force. Sarah envisioned communities that embrace simplicity and foster strong connections, where people find fulfillment in nurturing relationships and living in harmony with nature. Such communities could serve as models for balancing modern advancements with traditional values.

2. Embracing Structured Learning and Adaptability:

From her interactions with AI, Sarah recognized the value of structured learning and adaptability in personal and professional development. By adopting strategies similar to those used in AI, individuals can enhance their learning processes and achieve their goals more effectively. Sarah advocated for educational systems and personal development programs that emphasize iterative learning, feedback, and adaptability, preparing individuals to thrive in an ever-evolving world.

3. Balancing Innovation with Historical Awareness:

The interactive museum's lessons on civilization underscored the importance of balancing innovation with respect for historical context. Sarah envisioned a future where technological advancements are pursued with an awareness of their potential impacts on society and the environment. By integrating new ideas with lessons from the past, individuals and institutions can ensure that progress is both meaningful and responsible.

4. Addressing Psychological Barriers:

The labyrinth of fear had taught Sarah that confronting and managing psychological barriers is crucial for personal growth. She envisioned initiatives that provide support and resources for individuals struggling with anxiety and other fears, promoting mental health and resilience. By addressing these barriers, people can achieve greater well-being and contribute more effectively to their communities and society.

5. Promoting Environmental Stewardship:

Sarah's eco-simulation experience highlighted the need for integrating sustainable practices into technological and societal advancements. She envisioned a future where environmental stewardship is a core value, with individuals and organizations making conscious efforts to reduce waste, conserve resources, and protect ecosystems. By aligning progress with environmental sustainability, society can ensure a healthier planet for future generations.

6. Fostering Perseverance and Patience:

The skill-building modules demonstrated the rewards of perseverance and patience in achieving mastery. Sarah envisioned educational and professional environments that cultivate these qualities, encouraging individuals to embrace challenges and view failures as opportunities for growth. By fostering a culture of perseverance, society can achieve greater innovation and excellence.

A Call to Action

As Sarah concluded her journey, she felt a deep sense of purpose and responsibility. The insights gained from her experiences had equipped her with a vision for a more harmonious future, one where personal growth, technological advancement, and societal progress are intertwined with values of simplicity, sustainability, and resilience.

Sarah's story serves as a call to action for readers to reflect on their own journeys and consider how they can contribute to a better world. By integrating the lessons learned from village life, technology, civilization, and personal development, individuals can make meaningful contributions to a future marked by balance and fulfillment.

The journey through "Echoes of Tomorrow" had been a transformative one, offering a unique perspective on the interconnectedness of various aspects of life. As readers close the book, they are encouraged to carry forward the insights and values explored in Sarah's story, applying them to their own lives and contributing to a more harmonious and fulfilling world.

End of Epilogue

In this epilogue, Sarah's experiences are synthesized into a vision for the future, highlighting the interconnectedness of personal growth, technological advancement, and societal progress. The narrative emphasizes the importance of applying these lessons to create a more balanced and fulfilling world, inviting readers to reflect on their own roles in contributing to a harmonious future.

Glossary:

A glossary of 101 terms related to the themes and elements explored in your novel, *"Echoes of Tomorrow"*:

1. **Adaptability**: The ability to adjust to new conditions or changes in the environment.

2. **AI (Artificial Intelligence)**: Simulation of human intelligence in machines that are programmed to think and learn.

3. **Balance**: Equilibrium achieved between various aspects of life or systems, such as technological progress and environmental sustainability.

4. **Community**: A group of individuals living in proximity who share common values, interests, and support each other.

5. **Coping Strategies**: Techniques and methods used to manage stress, anxiety, and psychological challenges.

6. **Creativity**: The ability to create new ideas, concepts, or things that are original and valuable.

7. **Cybernetics**: The interdisciplinary study of the structure of regulatory systems, including feedback and control mechanisms in both machines and living organisms.

8. **Design Thinking**: A problem-solving approach that involves empathy, creativity, and iterative testing.

9. **Empathy**: The ability to understand and share the feelings of another person.

10. **Endurance**: The capacity to sustain prolonged physical or mental effort.

11. **Environmental Stewardship**: Responsible management and care of the natural environment through sustainable practices.

12. **Feedback**: Information received about performance or behavior that can be used to improve and adjust actions.

13. **Foresight**: The ability to anticipate future trends and potential challenges to make informed decisions.

14. **Holistic**: An approach that considers the whole system, including all interconnected parts, rather than focusing on individual components.

15. **Incremental Progress**: Gradual improvement achieved through small, step-by-step changes.

16. **Innovation**: The introduction of new ideas, methods, or products that improve upon existing ones.

17. **Interactive Dialogue**: A conversational exchange that involves active participation and engagement from all parties involved.

18. **Iterative Process**: A method of refining and improving through repeated cycles of testing and feedback.

19. **Mastery**: High-level proficiency and skill achieved through sustained effort and practice.

20. **Mindfulness**: The practice of being present and fully engaged in the moment, often used to manage stress and anxiety.

21. **Perseverance**: Continued effort and determination to achieve a goal despite difficulties and delays.

22. **Personal Growth**: The process of improving oneself through self-reflection, learning, and development.

23. **Resilience**: The capacity to recover quickly from difficulties and adapt to adversity.

24. **Sustainability**: The practice of using resources in a way that meets current needs without compromising future generations' ability to meet their own needs.

25. **Technology**: Tools, systems, and methods used to solve problems and improve human life, including digital and mechanical innovations.

26. **Tradition**: Established customs and practices passed down through generations that influence cultural and societal norms.

27. **Transformation**: Significant change that alters the state or nature of something, often leading to improvement or development.

28. **Values**: Core beliefs and principles that guide behavior and decision-making.

29. **Village Life**: The lifestyle and community dynamics characteristic of rural, small-scale, and close-knit communities.

30. **Well-being**: A state of overall health, happiness, and life satisfaction.

31. **Algorithm**: A step-by-step procedure or formula for solving a problem or performing a task, commonly used in computing.

32. **Automation**: The use of technology to perform tasks with minimal human intervention.

33. **Biodiversity**: The variety of life forms in a given area, including plants, animals, and microorganisms, essential for ecosystem health.

34. **Cognitive Restructuring**: A therapeutic technique that involves changing negative thought patterns to improve emotional responses.

35. **Cultural Heritage**: The legacy of physical artifacts and intangible attributes inherited from past generations.

36. **Decision-Making**: The process of making choices by identifying and evaluating options and selecting the most appropriate one.

37. **Digital Literacy**: The ability to effectively use digital tools and technologies for various purposes.

38. **Ecosystem**: A biological community of interacting organisms and their physical environment.

39. **Ethics**: Moral principles that govern behavior and decision-making.

40. **Feedback Loop**: A system where outputs are fed back into the system as inputs to influence future behavior or performance.

41. **Game Theory**: The study of mathematical models of strategic interaction among rational decision-makers.

42. **Historical Context**: The circumstances and events surrounding a particular historical period that influence its significance.

43. **Human-Centered Design**: An approach to design that prioritizes the needs, experiences, and perspectives of end-users.

44. **Iterative Testing**: Repeatedly testing and refining a product or process to improve its functionality and effectiveness.

45. **Lifestyle**: The way in which a person or community lives, including habits, attitudes, and cultural practices.

46. **Mindful Awareness**: The practice of paying attention to one's thoughts, feelings, and surroundings in a non-judgmental way.

47. **Natural Resources**: Materials and substances provided by nature that are used by humans, such as water, minerals, and forests.

48. **Optimization**: The process of making something as effective or functional as possible by refining and improving.

49. **Pattern Recognition**: The ability to identify and understand patterns or trends within data or experiences.

50. **Personal Development**: Activities and practices aimed at enhancing one's skills, knowledge, and overall personal growth.

51. **Productivity**: The efficiency of producing goods or services, often measured by output per unit of input.

52. **Proactive**: Taking initiative and anticipating potential issues before they arise.

53. **Resource Management**: The efficient and effective use of resources to achieve desired outcomes.

54. **Scenario Planning**: A strategic method for envisioning different future scenarios and preparing for potential outcomes.

55. **Social Dynamics**: The patterns of behavior and interaction within a social group or community.

56. **Strategic Thinking**: The ability to plan and make decisions based on long-term goals and potential future scenarios.

57. **Sustainability Practices**: Actions and strategies aimed at reducing negative environmental impacts and promoting long-term ecological balance.

58. **Systemic Change**: Transformations that address underlying structures and processes to improve systems or organizations.

59. **Time Management**: The process of planning and controlling how much time to spend on specific activities.

60. **Tradition vs. Innovation**: The balance between preserving established practices and embracing new ideas and technologies.

61. **User Experience (UX)**: The overall experience and satisfaction of users when interacting with a product or system.

62. **Virtual Reality (VR)**: A simulated environment created by computer technology that immerses users in a digital experience.

63. **Well-Being Metrics**: Measures used to assess various aspects of an individual's or community's overall health and satisfaction.

64. **Workflow Optimization**: Improving the efficiency and effectiveness of processes and tasks within a workflow.

65. **Agile Methodology**: A flexible and iterative approach to project management and software development.

66. **Bioethics**: The study of ethical issues related to biological and medical research and practices.

67. **Climate Change**: Long-term alterations in temperature, precipitation, and other climate patterns resulting from human activity and natural processes.

68. **Crisis Management**: Strategies and actions taken to address and mitigate the impact of a crisis or emergency situation.

69. **Data Analytics**: The process of analyzing and interpreting data to make informed decisions and identify trends.

70. **E-Governance**: The use of digital technologies to improve the efficiency, transparency, and accessibility of government services.

71. **Ethnography**: The study and systematic recording of human cultures and societies through observation and interaction.

72. **Feedback Mechanism**: A system that uses feedback to influence and adjust processes or behaviors.

73. **Gamification**: The application of game-design elements and principles to non-game contexts to engage and motivate users.

74. **Holistic Education**: An educational approach that addresses the intellectual, emotional, social, and physical aspects of students.

75. **Impact Assessment**: The evaluation of the potential effects and consequences of a project, policy, or action.

76. **Integrated Systems**: Systems that combine various components and processes to function as a cohesive whole.

77. **Life Cycle Analysis**: The assessment of the environmental impact of a product or service throughout its entire life cycle.

78. **Mind-Body Connection**: The relationship between mental and physical health, emphasizing how they influence each other.

79. **Participatory Design**: An approach that involves users and stakeholders in the design process to ensure their needs are met.

80. **Predictive Analytics**: The use of statistical techniques and algorithms to predict future trends and behaviors.

81. **Risk Management**: The identification, assessment, and prioritization of risks followed by coordinated efforts to minimize their impact.

82. **Scenario Simulation:** The creation of simulations to explore and evaluate different potential outcomes and scenarios.

83. **Stakeholder Engagement:** The process of involving individuals and groups who are affected by or have an interest in a project or decision.

84. **Sustainable Development:** Economic development that aims to meet current needs without compromising the ability of future generations to meet their own needs.

85. **Systems Thinking:** An approach that examines how different components of a system interact and influence each other.

86. **Technology Integration:** The process of incorporating technology into existing systems and workflows to enhance functionality and efficiency.

87. **Transformation Management:** The strategies and practices used to guide and manage significant organizational or societal changes.

88. **User-Centered Design:** Design principles that prioritize the needs and experiences of users in creating products and services.

89. **Value Proposition:** The unique value that a product or service offers to its users or customers.

90. **Virtual Simulation:** The use of virtual environments to replicate real-world scenarios for training or experimentation.

91. **Waste Reduction:** Strategies and practices aimed at minimizing the generation of waste and improving resource efficiency.

92. **Wellness Programs:** Initiatives and activities designed to promote physical, mental, and emotional health.

93. **Cultural Sensitivity:** Awareness and respect for cultural differences and practices in interactions and decision-making.

94. **Design Iteration:** The process of refining and improving a design through repeated cycles of feedback and modification.

95. **Empowerment:** The process of providing individuals or communities with the tools, resources, and confidence to take control of their lives.

96. **Humanitarian Efforts:** Actions and initiatives aimed at improving the well-being and quality of life for people in need.

97. **Innovation Ecosystem:** A network of organizations, individuals, and resources that collaborate to foster and support innovation.

98. ***Knowledge Sharing***: The practice of exchanging information, skills, and expertise among individuals or groups.

99. ***Leadership Development***: Programs and activities designed to enhance leadership skills and capabilities.

100. ***Outcome-Based Evaluation:*** Assessing the results and impact of a program or initiative based on its objectives and goals.

101. ***Visionary Thinking***: The ability to envision and plan for future possibilities and opportunities beyond the present.

This glossary provides definitions and explanations for terms relevant to the themes of village life, technology, civilization, and personal development explored in your novel. Each term is designed to enhance understanding and provide context for the concepts discussed.

Epilogue: A Harmonious Future

Sarah: *[Standing at the edge of the interactive museum, reflecting on her journey]* "I can hardly believe how much I've learned. Each chapter of my journey has intertwined so many aspects of life—village simplicity, AI learning, civilization's evolution, and personal growth. It feels like everything has come together in a beautiful mosaic."

Curator: *[Joining Sarah]* "It's fascinating how different experiences can converge to form a cohesive understanding of the world. The insights you've gained highlight the interconnectedness of various aspects of human life."

Sarah: "Absolutely. I remember the village life, where simplicity and connection were central. It was a place where time seemed to slow down, and every interaction was meaningful. What I learned there about the importance of community and living in harmony with nature has stayed with me."

Elder: *[Echoing Sarah's thoughts]* "In our village, we live by the principle that fulfillment comes from nurturing relationships and embracing simplicity. The natural world and our community are integral to our sense of well-being."

Sarah: "Then there was the AI research lab, where I saw how machines learn and adapt. Dr. Liam explained how AI's learning processes are similar to human strategies—breaking tasks into steps, learning from feedback, and iterative progress. It made me realize how these strategies can be applied to our own learning journeys."

Dr. Liam: *[Nodding in agreement]* "Exactly. By understanding AI's adaptability, we can improve our approach to personal and professional growth. Persistence and structured approaches are key to both machine learning and human development."

Sarah: "The museum's interactive timeline was another eye-opener. Seeing the evolution of civilization through different epochs and understanding how small, thoughtful changes can have a profound impact was enlightening."

Curator: "Advancing civilization responsibly involves balancing innovation with historical awareness. It's about embracing new technologies while respecting and learning from the past. Your choices during the interactive scenarios demonstrated how incremental changes can shape a better future."

Sarah: "And then there was the labyrinth of fears. Navigating through that VR simulation made me confront my own anxieties and understand various coping strategies like mindfulness and cognitive restructuring."

Guide: [Offering insight] "Fear can indeed be paralyzing, but confronting it is crucial for personal growth. Techniques like gradual exposure and understanding the root of your fears can help you build resilience and manage anxiety."

Sarah: "The eco-simulation was another significant experience. Experimenting with sustainable practices and interacting with virtual ecosystems underscored the importance of environmental stewardship."

Eco-Expert: [Affirming] "Integrating sustainable practices and respecting natural processes is vital. Even small actions, such as reducing waste and conserving resources, can lead to significant improvements in preserving our environment."

Sarah: "Lastly, the skill-building modules emphasized the value of perseverance and patience. The mentor's advice about the importance of sustained effort and avoiding shortcuts was particularly resonant."

Mentor: "Mastery and true excellence come from dedication and time. Quick fixes may offer temporary results, but sustained effort and learning from failures lead to lasting success."

Sarah: [Reflecting on the lessons learned] "All these experiences have combined to offer a holistic understanding of how different elements of life are interconnected. From village life's simplicity to AI's structured learning, civilization's balance, and personal growth, everything contributes to a more harmonious future."

Curator: "Indeed, your journey has illustrated how personal growth, technological advancements, and societal progress are intertwined with values of simplicity, sustainability, and resilience. It's a call to action for all of us."

Sarah: "I feel a profound sense of purpose. It's clear that by embracing simplicity, adopting structured learning, balancing innovation with historical context, addressing psychological barriers, promoting environmental stewardship, and fostering perseverance, we can create a more balanced and fulfilling world."

Eco-Expert: "Exactly. Every action counts. By integrating these insights into our lives and communities, we can contribute to a more harmonious and sustainable future."

Mentor: "Remember, the journey doesn't end here. The principles and values you've learned are tools for ongoing growth and contribution."

Sarah: [Nodding with determination] "I'm ready to carry forward these lessons and apply them to my life and work. It's up to each of us to make a difference and build a better world."

Curator: "And that's the essence of your journey—using your newfound understanding to inspire and enact positive change."

Sarah: "Thank you to everyone who has guided me along the way. Each step of this journey has been transformative, and I'm excited to see how these insights will shape my future and the future of those around me."

Guide: "You've embraced the journey with openness and curiosity. Now, take these lessons and let them guide your path."

Sarah: [As she prepares to leave] "Here's to a harmonious future, where simplicity, innovation, sustainability, and personal growth come together to create a better world for all."

Epilogue Concludes

In closing, Sarah's exploration through "Echoes of Tomorrow" has been a transformative experience, merging diverse themes into a cohesive vision for a more balanced and fulfilling world. The novel's interactive and immersive elements have provided readers with valuable insights into the interconnectedness of village life, technology, civilization, and personal development. As Sarah's journey comes to an end, it serves as a reminder that every aspect of life contributes to the broader goal of creating a harmonious and sustainable future.

Haiku for "Echoes of Tomorrow"

Chapter 1: The Village Canvas

1. Cobblestone whispers,
   Sunrise over quiet fields—
   Ancient rhythms hum.

2. Gentle morning light,
   Children play beneath the trees,
   Time drifts in their wake.

3. Elder's wisdom flows,
   Through the threads of village life,
   Peace in every breath.

4. Ripe fruit on the vine,
   Community gathers round,
   Harvest of warm smiles.

5. Soft winds through the grass,
   Simple life, profound content,
   Echoes of the past.

6. Laughter in the air,
   Songs of ancestors linger,
   Traditions endure.

7. By the hearth they sit,
   Stories woven through the night,
   Connection and warmth.

8. Fields of golden grain,
   Hands toil with love and purpose,
   Nature's gentle hand.

9. Moonlight on still ponds,
   Reflections of ancient ways,
   Silent harmony.

10. Softly spoken words,
    In the quiet of the dawn,
    Trust in every gaze.

11. Paths of stone and earth,
Footsteps echo timeless songs,
Village life endures.

12. Warmth of shared embrace,
In the simplicity of,
Community's grace.

13. Crickets in the dusk,
Songs of village life unfold,
Evening's calm sigh.

14. Sun sets on the hills,
Shadows lengthen, hearts find peace,
Day's end softly calls.

15. Gentle hands at work,
Crafting dreams from simple means,
Life's beauty revealed.

16. Winding village lanes,
Stories etched in every turn,
History's soft voice.

17. The old oak stands firm,
Guardian of time and tales,
Roots deep in the past.

18. Harvest moon above,
Fields bathed in soft, silver light,
Night whispers of calm.

19. Day's end, twilight's hush,
Families gather, hearts warm,
Shared moments of grace.

20. Nature's gentle touch,
In every leaf and whisper,
Village life unfolds.

Chapter 2: AI's Learning Symphony

21. Algorithms dance,
Patterns weave through silicon,
Learning's quiet hum.

22. Data streams like light,
Machines mimic human thought,
Patterns in the code.

23. Steps broken down small,
Iterative progress made,
Learning's quiet path.

24. Feedback shapes the path,
AI learns from each attempt,
Growth in every line.

25. Complexity
Simplified by algorithms,
Learning in the flow.

26. Structured, step by step,
AI's mind adapts with ease,
Human parallels.

27. Simulations rise,
Virtual worlds come to life,
Learning through the game.

28. Adaptive minds bloom,
Machines mirror human growth,
Patterns come to play.

29. Goals broken to steps,
Iterative learning's key,
Persistence wins out.

30. Data's silent song,
Teaching machines to understand,
Patterns in the dark.

31. Feedback loops refine,
Each error a lesson learned,
Machines grow with time.

32. Virtual insights,
Simulations teach us much,
Lessons for us all.

33. Structured pathways shine,
AI's growth in every step,
Humans mirror this.

34. Patterns in the code,
Learning from each iteration,
Machines find their way.

35. Systems evolve fast,
Learning curves in digital,
Growth in every byte.

36. Machines think in steps,
Humans also grow this way,
Learning's common thread.

37. From data, wisdom,
AI learns to adapt well,
Structured, step by step.

38. Algorithm's grace,
Mimicking human insight,
Growth in every line.

39. Progress in the code,
Learning from each simulation,
Steps lead to new paths.

40. Virtual world grows,
Learning through each simulation,
Steps in AI's dance.

Chapter 3: Civilization's Mosaic

41. Epochs unfold wide,
Timeline's stories interweave,
History's soft hum.

42. Innovations rise,
Balance with the past we seek,
Lessons guide our way.

43. From old to new paths,
Small changes shift the future,
Civility grows.

44. Timelines stretch so far,
Each era's lessons are clear,
Change in every age.

45. Historical threads,
Woven into future's cloth,
Guidance from the past.

46. Echoes through the years,
Small actions shape grand designs,
History's soft voice.

47. Interactive sights,
Lessons from the ages blend,
Mosaic of time.

48. Past and future dance,
Timeless lessons guide our steps,
Balance in our hands.

49. Change is slow but sure,
Lessons learned from ages past,
Future's path is clear.

50. Epochs speak to us,
Each moment builds the future,
History's own song.

51. Through time's shifting lens,
Civilization's path,
Guided by the past.

52. Innovations blend,
With history's gentle touch,
Future's form revealed.

53. Small changes echo,
In the grand sweep of history,
Future's shape takes form.

54. Past informs the now,
History's lessons guide us,
Future's clear path blooms.

55. Interactive paths,
Civilization's dance,
Lessons from the ages.

56. Past and future meet,
Timeless wisdom shapes our way,
Change in every step.

57. Ages intertwine,
Lessons from the past remain,
Guide for future steps.

58. From past to future,
Small changes lead the way forward,
History's embrace.

59. Evolution's thread,
Weaving past with future's hopes,
Balance in our hands.

60. Interactive tales,
Timeless lessons blend with now,
Future's path revealed.

Chapter 4: The Labyrinth of Fear

61. Fear's dark maze unfurls,
Navigating through the unknown,
Courage lights the path.

62. VR shadows loom,
Facing fears, confronting doubts,
Strength in every step.

63. Mindfulness reveals,
Roots of fears and hidden doubts,
Peace in gentle breaths.

64. Exposure brings light,
Gradual steps lead to calm,
Fear's grip starts to fade.

65. Cognitive shifts,
Restructuring the mind's maze,
New pathways emerge.

66. Labyrinth's dark twists,
Courage found in every turn,
Fear meets its own end.

67. Shadows whisper soft,
Fear's grip tightens then releases,
Strength in every step.

68. Gradual exposure,
Fears faced in small, steady steps,
Courage grows within.

69. Mind's maze unfolds wide,
Confronting fears with clear insight,
Peace in every turn.

70. Fear's edges soften,
Facing the unknown with grace,
Strength in every breath.

71. Confronting dark fears,
Virtual pathways reveal,
Strength in each step found.

72. Cognitive light,
Restructuring the mind's maze,
Fear's shadows retreat.

73. Gradual light shines,
Fears met with steady, soft steps,
Strength in each small win.

74. Labyrinth of fears,
Navigated with brave heart,
Peace in every step.

75. Mindful courage grows,
Facing fears with gentle breath,
Strength in every move.

76. Shadows in the maze,
Fears met with patient resolve,
Strength in quiet steps.

77. Exposure's soft light,
Fears faced with courage and care,
Peace in every turn.

78. Cognitive change,
Restructuring the dark maze,
Light in every step.

79. VR's dark maze shows,
Fears faced with strength and insight,
Peace in every move.

80. Confronting fears now,
Labyrinth of the unknown,
Strength in each small win.

Chapter 5: The Symphony of Mastery

81. Skills honed through practice,
Patience forms the path to strength,
Mastery takes time.

82. Effort's steady path,
Perseverance guides the way,
Excellence revealed.

83. Shortcuts fade away,
Dedication builds the road,
True mastery blooms.

84. Challenges faced hard,
Steady steps forge excellence,
Success through patience.

85. Discipline's quiet,
Crafting skills with gentle care,
Mastery's own song.

86. Practice's soft hum,
Effort shapes the path to skill,
Excellence revealed.

87. Perseverance strong,
Patience weaves the fabric fine,
Mastery unfolds.

88. Skills grow with each try,
Dedication's steady hand,
Success's soft glow.

89. Long paths of practice,
Skill's grace forms through steady work,
Mastery's own song.

90. Quick fixes falter,
True strength in sustained effort,
Mastery awaits.

91. *Steady hands at work,*
Skill's journey through patience's path,
Success in each step.

92. *Effort's steady beat,*
Skills honed through unwavering drive,
Mastery's embrace.

93. *Patience builds the path,*
Skills emerge through steady work,
Excellence achieved.

94. *Dedication's path,*
Crafting skills with quiet grace,
Mastery's own song.

95. *Long hours refine skill,*
Patience weaves a path to strength,
Mastery's reward.

96. *Practice's soft voice,*
Effort shapes the road to skill,
Success in every step.

97. *Perseverance's touch,*
Skills evolve through steady care,
Mastery's own form.

98. *Skills honed through the night,*
Patience guides each careful step,
Excellence achieved.

99. *Dedication's grace,*
Crafting skill through steady work,
Mastery's own song.

100. *Effort's steady pulse,*
Skills refined through practice's path,
Success through patience.

Chapter 6: Khudrat (The Nature)

101. *Nature's soft embrace,*
Virtual worlds reflect truth,
Harmony in touch.

102. Ecosystems thrive,
Sustainability's call,
Future's path unfolds.

103. Gentle green of life,
Small actions lead to great change,
Nature's quiet song.

104. Respect for the earth,
Harmony in every step,
Sustainability's grace.

105. Virtual forests,
Teachings of nature's own ways,
Balance in our hands.

106. Future's bright with green,
Conserving, caring for life,
Nature's gentle touch.

107. Nature's voice speaks soft,
In every leaf and whisper,
Harmony revealed.

108. Simulations show,
Interconnectedness,
Nature's quiet hum.

109. Small changes in care,
Impact the world in great ways,
Nature's call is clear.

110. Eco-friendly paths,
Virtual lessons guide us,
Future's green embrace.

111. Nature's hand guides us,
Through virtual ecosystems,
Sustainability.

112. Environmental,
Lessons from the virtual,
Harmony achieved.

113. Digital forests,
Nature's patterns mirrored true,
Sustainability's path.

114.   *Green futures arise,*
Conservation's quiet path,
Nature's soft embrace.

115.   *Simulations teach,*
Eco-friendly practices,
Future's path revealed.

116.   *Nature's gentle voice,*
Echoes through the virtual,
Balance in our hands.

117.   *Virtual streams flow,*
Lessons in conserving life,
Nature's calm whisper.

118.   *Green lessons unfold,*
Digital worlds teach us much,
Future's path is clear.

119.   *Ecosystems blend,*
Virtual lessons reveal,
Nature's quiet grace.

120.   *Small actions lead change,*
Sustainability's call,
Nature's voice is heard.

Chapter 7: The Journey of Mastery

121.   *Skill's long, winding road,*
Patience and effort entwine,
Mastery unfolds.

122.   *Dedication's pulse,*
Perseverance lights the way,
Excellence achieved.

123.   *Crafting through long nights,*
Skill refined by steady hand,
Mastery's own song.

124.   *Shortcuts lose their shine,*
True strength in effort's embrace,
Mastery awaits.

125. Steady, patient hands,
Skill's journey through practice's path,
Success's own glow.

126. Effort's quiet beat,
Skills emerge through patient work,
Mastery revealed.

127. Challenges faced hard,
Dedication's steady path,
Excellence unfolds.

128. Practice shapes the way,
Patience builds the path to skill,
Mastery's own song.

129. Long hours refine skill,
Effort's steady, gentle path,
Success through patience.

130. Perseverance's grace,
Crafting skill with quiet care,
Mastery's embrace.

131. Skills honed through hard work,
Dedication's steady hand,
Mastery achieved.

132. Effort's guiding light,
Skills emerge through patience's path,
Success in each step.

133. Patience builds the path,
Skill's journey through steady care,
Mastery unfolds.

134. Crafting through long nights,
Skill refined by patient hands,
Success's own glow.

135. Dedication's path,
Effort shapes the road to skill,
Mastery revealed.

136. Skills grow through each try,
Perseverance guides the way,
Success through patience.

137. Steady hands craft skill,
Mastery blooms through effort,
Excellence achieved.

138. Patience and hard work,
Skills emerge through steady care,
Mastery's own song.

139. Effort's steady hand,
Crafting skill through practice's path,
Success in each step.

140. Long hours refine skill,
Dedication's gentle touch,
Mastery's reward.

Epilogue: A Harmonious Future

141. Journey's end draws near,
Lessons blend in harmony,
Future's path revealed.

142. Village, tech, and more,
Mosaic of life's grand weave,
Harmony in sight.

143. Insights guide the way,
Simple truths and complex paths,
Future's bright embrace.

144. Lessons from the past,
Future's path in gentle hands,
Harmony achieved.

145. Knowledge intertwined,
From village to AI's core,
Future's song unfolds.

146. Interconnected,
Insights shape the world anew,
Harmony's own light.

147. Paths of wisdom blend,
Simple truths guide us forward,
Future's grace revealed.

148. Insights from the past,
Technology's bright future,
Harmony achieved.

149. Future's bright embrace,
Lessons learned and paths revealed,
Harmony's own song.

150. Journey's end is here,
Understanding's light shines bright,
Future's path in sight.

151. Echoes of the past,
Guiding us to futures new,
Harmony revealed.

152. Knowledge shapes our path,
Lessons blend in perfect grace,
Future's bright embrace.

153. Interwoven threads,
Past and future merge as one,
Harmony achieved.

154. Insight guides the way,
Simple truths and complex paths,
Future's bright embrace.

155. Past and future blend,
Mosaic of life's grand weave,
Harmony in sight.

156. Knowledge intertwines,
Village life and tech advance,
Future's path revealed.

157. Lessons from the past,
Guiding through the future's light,
Harmony achieved.

158. Echoes softly blend,
Past and future merge with grace,
Harmony revealed.

159. Future's bright and clear,
Insights from the journey guide,
Harmony achieved.

160.   *Mosaic of life,*
Lessons blend in future's light,
Harmony revealed.

This collection of haikus aims to capture the essence of each chapter in the novel, weaving together the interconnected themes of village life, AI learning, civilization's evolution, personal mastery, environmental stewardship, and a harmonious future. Each haiku serves as a reflective snapshot, creating a poetic tapestry that mirrors the novel's journey.

www.ingramcontent.com/pod-product-compliance
Lightning Source LLC
Chambersburg PA
CBHW062108220526
45471CB00010B/3657